AN ANARCHY OF CHILIES

AN ANARCHY OF CHILIES

CAZ HILDEBRAND

Thames & Hudson

Contents

Introduction

For millennia, chillies have been cultivated for flavour and flame.

WHERE HERBS ARE generally green and leafy, and spices are dried seeds, roots, arils or bark, chillies are brightly multi-coloured pepper pods – horticulturally speaking, fruits – picked at varying stages of ripeness and used either fresh or dried. There are hundreds of herb and spice species but only five domesticated chilli pepper species (with twenty-six known wild ones), which riotously yield thousands of radically different cultivars, from the sweet bell pepper to the mortifying Carolina Reaper.

The chilli pepper – 'chilli' from the Aztec Nahuatl language, 'pepper' because Christopher Columbus and his crew wrongly thought the fiery plant was a relative of spicy black pepper – belongs to the Capsicum genus, which is part of the not-so-deadly nightshade (Solanaceae) family. Cousins include tomatoes, aubergine (eggplant), potatoes, petunias and goji berries – a remarkably dissimilar bunch, bar the fact they all share the same green hat-like stem, or peduncle. Chilli plants grow variously: the average height is less than 1 m (3 ft), though a few tower at 9 m (30 ft). The pods range from long and thin to round, oblate or bell-like in shape, with green, yellow or white colouration when immature, ripening to red, orange, brown and any shade between. Most plants are ready for picking after 70 days and the pods are fully ripened after 130 days. Today chillies are grown especially in China, Indonesia, Korea, Mexico, Nigeria and Turkey, though one of the hottest new chillies – the Naga Viper (see pages 202–03) – was cultivated in Cumbria, England, and its distinctive character attributed to the wet climate.

Chillies, of course, are prized for their 'heat' – and have been ever since they were first gathered and eaten in Mexico around 7000 BCE. Mesoamericans began to cultivate chilli plants between 5200 and 3400 BCE. The Aztecs used chilli to season a sacred drink called *cacahuatl*, a mixture of cocoa beans, corn, chilli peppers, pimiento, vanilla beans, water and spices (the earliest hot chocolate). In the West, little was known about chillies before the 1490s, when Christopher Columbus brought chilli plants back to Spain from the Caribbean – along with turkeys, pineapples and hammocks.

Chillies then spread like wildfire throughout Europe, from Spain and Portugal outward. When the Ottoman Turks invaded Hungary in 1526 they took their chillies with them, triggering the Hungarian penchant for paprika; by 1699, 33 chillies were listed in the English herbal *Plantarum historiae universalis Oxoniensis* by Robert Morison, botanist to Charles II. After reaching India, Africa and South East Asia, many new chilli varieties were cultivated to satisfy the growing appetite for intensely hot food inspired by the international spice trade. Today it is impossible to imagine a *laksa* without the heat of chilli, so it is interesting to note the fairly recent conversion of Thai and Indonesian cuisine to heat.

Chillies are 'hot' because they contain capsaicin, an alkaloid found in the pepper's flesh, especially concentrated in the white interior ribs that bear the seeds. From an evolutionary point of view, capsaicin acts as a deterrent against ingestion of the plant by mammals, and also inhibits the spread of fungal infections by insects. Chillies' successful natural dissemination is partly down to the fact that birds are not sensitive to capsaicin and can happily eat the hottest chilli without effect, distributing the seeds on the wing. In humans, capsaicin chemically stimulates TRPV1 (pronounced trip-vee-one) receptors in different parts of the mouth, from the throat and tongue to the mid- and back palate. Varying amounts and positions of TRPV1 receptors explain why chilli 'mouthfeel' and tolerance for heat varies so much from person to person. And perhaps the most fascinating thing: TRPV1 passes to the brain through nerves that communicate the sense of touch, not taste. Chillies have tastes and smells, yes, but they are first and foremost culinary instruments of touch. And because of this, of course: the potential for pain.

The heat of chillies is expressed in Scoville Heat Units (SHUs), based on a test developed in 1912 in which extracts of chillies dissolved in alcohol were diluted with sugar water until the capsaicin was no longer detected: the greater the dilution, the greater the SHUs (the hottest chillies reach millions of SHUs). Macho chilliheads have come to dominate the chilli world with their hunger for the hottest; seeking out and eating 'superhots' with every intention of getting 'burned up' (chilli parlance for experiencing hiccoughing, sweating, ear-popping, abdominal cramps and/or vomiting after excessive consumption). Meanwhile, everyday chilli lovers claim that peppers wake up their palates to other flavours, though the less convinced argue that chilli heat distorts accompanying tastes. For most chilli lovers, it seems, the wild sensations are the point: a way of enjoying the body's negative responses to danger, akin to going on white-knuckle rollercoaster rides and watching scary movies. And I do wonder if the thing really craved is the absence of pain after the chilli. Like the silence after a poem that seems to have been the point all along, chillies engage our desire not only for survival, but also for rejuvenation.

Eating chillies is not quite the Russian roulette game of sampling the mouth-numbing Japanese delicacy *fugu* – the pufferfish that really can kill you if you get a shoddy chef – but it is somewhere close. There is no official measurement of chilli heat levels, and the amount of capsaicin in individual chillies of the same type can vary dramatically. For this reason, SHU values for chillies are usually expressed as a range, and in the anarchic chilli world different experts give different highs and lows. In this book we've tried to chart a consensus on the SHU ranges, but it's best to take a tiny taste and judge each chilli for yourself before committing to the whole pod. There are always a few very milk-mild or lava-hot outliers, and unpredictable heat is part of the fun of the chilli experience.

The 100 chillies profiled in this book have been chosen to showcase their impressive range of shape, colour, flavour and heat. Rather than illustrate them in the refined tradition of botanical art, or use photography that – however brilliant – can somehow miss the chilli's personality, I have represented our selection using a contemporary light-touch graphic design style and technique inspired by four-colour or process printing. CMYK – the letters stand for the colours cyan, magenta, yellow and black – is a standard, universally used printing technique that creates the full spectrum of colours and tones by combining varying amounts of these four coloured inks (yellow and magenta when overlaid, for instance, combine to produce red). The layering of only these four colours enables me to depict each chilli's unique vibrancy and shape with both depth and transparency. Process printing is the perfect analogy for the profligate variations of chillies, themselves all hybrids or cross-pollinated from only a very limited palette of the original species.

Why 'an anarchy of chillies?' For many reasons. There is something defiantly anarchic in their fire and burn. What other natural ingredients in our food can truly provide that revolutionary power? Additionally, in the growing of capsicum plants, open-pollination can yield an anarchy of hybridization in the absence of a smart seed producer to isolate certain varieties: this is a boistrous botanical bunch that just wants to survive and thrive at all costs. This also explains their impressive longevity. Chillies began as small spherical fruits many thousands of years ago – see the Chiltepín entry (see pages 164–65) – and have since branched out in all kinds of wondrous ways, shapes and dispositions. In this awe-inspiring range of forms there is a sort of creative anarchy at work.

Finally, and true to the root of the word 'anarchy' itself, the chilli kingdom has no leaders. There is no official chilli pepper governing body, no decree as to which superhot is hottest – and the next one is always about to arrive – and no consensus as to whether heat, flavour, colour or shape is most important. The invitation, then, is to enter this wild and wonderful world, best foot forward, enjoy chillies for a multiplicity of reasons, and be renewed and revivified.

CAZ HILDEBRAND

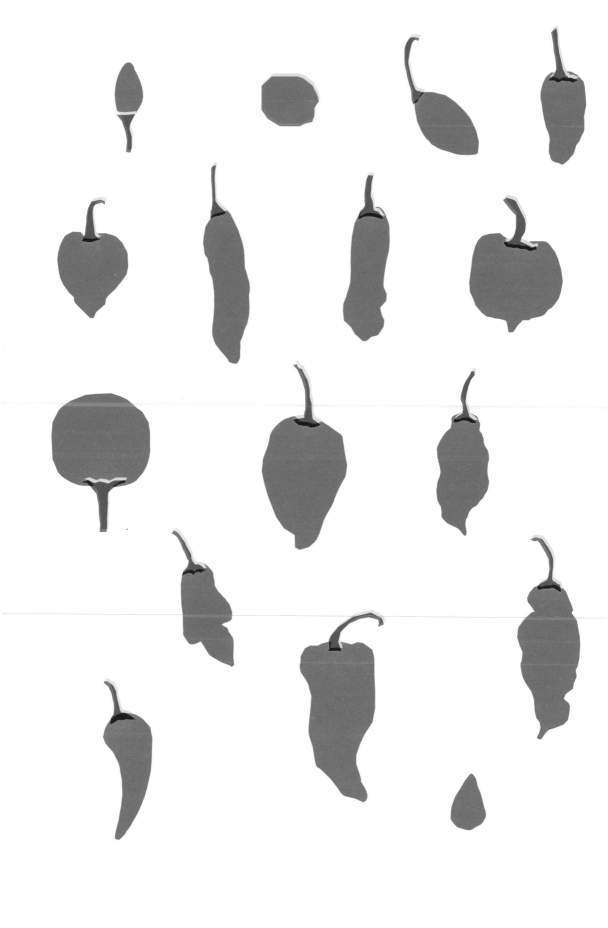

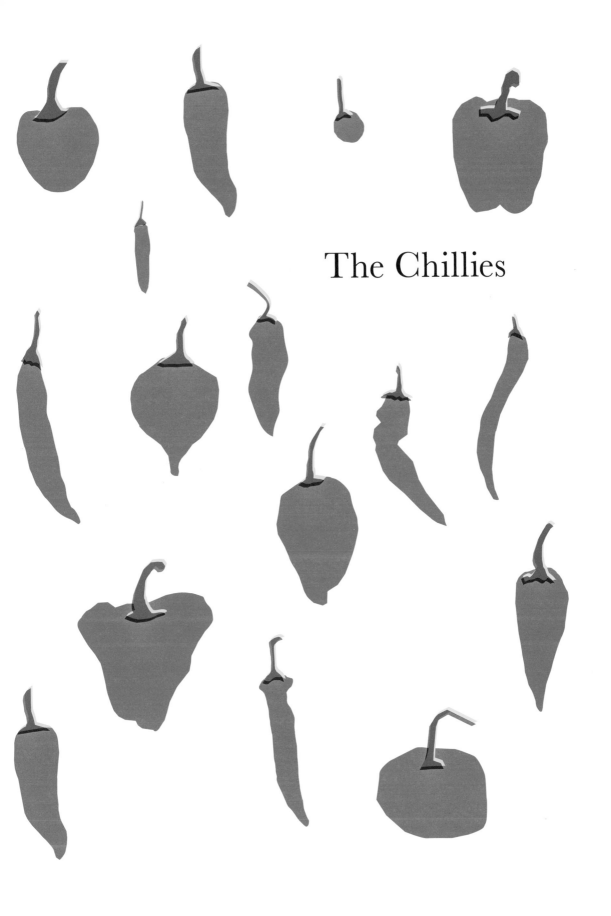

The Chillies

Capsicum annuum

Bell

SIZE
10 × 5 cm (4 × 2 in.)

ORIGIN
Mexico, central America,
northern South America

GROW
The plants produce 10–20
pods with glistening green
leaves. The Ace Hybrid is
a beautifully shaped bell
cultivar.

EAT
Stuff (parboil first), fry, roast
or grill. Use in casseroles,
salads, soups, relishes,
crudités and sauces.

A SWEET PEPPER, first recorded in late seventeenth-century Panama, this is now the most economically important pepper in the world, with at least 200 cultivars. Despite a recessive gene that eliminates capsaicin, and therefore heat, these blocky, bell-shaped peppers with rounded edges are still members of the anarchic and extended chilli family, sharing the species name *Capsicum annuum* with many fiery siblings in what is the largest and most diverse chilli group.

What the bell pepper lacks in heat it makes up for in sturdy and attractive architecture, with a crispy, meaty texture and glossy skin in colours ranging from red, yellow and green to orange, purple, brown, black and ivory. It has great flavour, tangy and fruity, and high levels of vitamin C, particularly in red varieties. Interestingly, the bell pepper contains methoxypyrazine compounds found in Bordeaux-family wines such as Cabernet Sauvignon, Sauvignon Blanc and Malbec – look out for wine labels that talk about 'bell pepper' or 'herbal' notes.

Stuff it: stuffed bell peppers have a long history in many different traditional cuisines around the world: in Spain, *pimientos rellenos de arroz* (stuffed with saffron-flavoured rice and cooked in tomato sauce); in India, *bharwan shimla mirch* (stuffed with spiced mashed potatoes); in Denmark, *fyldte peberfrugter* (stuffed with bulgur wheat, mushrooms and kale); in Romania, *ardei umpluti* (stuffed with pork and rice and served in a sour cream sauce).

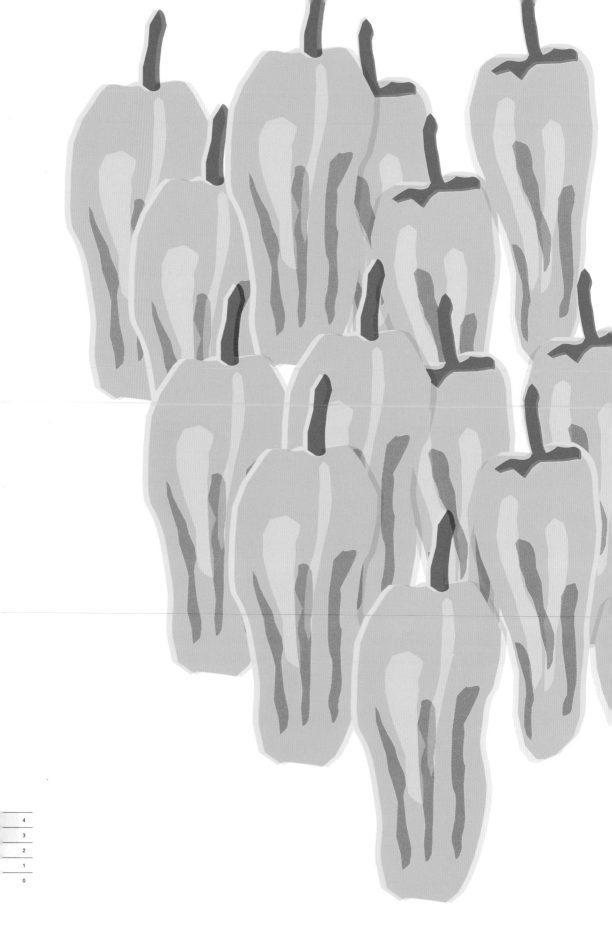

Capsicum annuum

Petit Marseillais

SCOVILLE HEAT UNITS 0 – 500

SIZE
10 × 4 cm (4 × 1½ in.)

ORIGIN
France

GROW
Tight, compact plants grow up to 60 cm (2 ft), great for growing in pots. This plant can tolerate dryness and heat, but prefers to be watered moderately.

EAT
Turn into sauces or chop into salads. Mix into a medley of vegetables slowly braised in olive oil – the traditional cooking technique of Provence. Pickle.

A SWEET AND SUNNY French heirloom pepper plant hailing from Provence in the south of France, the long, blocky, wavy, thin-skinned fruits – with their fantastic curves – ripen to a warm sunset-orange colour. American food historian William Woys Weaver is a big Petit Marseillais fan who was introduced to the 'brilliant wrinkled yellow peppers' by Owen Taylor of the Philadelphia Seed Exchange. In Provence the pods are picked green, stuffed with Gruyère cheese, eggs, garlic and parsley, seasoned, and then sautéed whole in olive oil. Although Petit Marseillais is considered a sweet pepper, I wanted to include it because France is not widely known for its capsicum varieties, and because of the pepper's fantastic flavour: surprising citrusy heat and aromatic, spicy undertones of tangerine.

Capsicum annuum

Pepperoncini

SCOVILLE HEAT UNITS 100 – 500

SIZE
7 x 2 cm (2¾ × ¾ in.)

ORIGIN
Italy

GROW
Mature plants grow up
to 60 cm (2 ft). Smaller
containers, such as window
boxes, can be used to grow
them.

EAT
Practise your appetizer
skills: fill with cream
cheese, bacon and cheddar;
or pancetta, anchovies,
mozzarella and basil; or even
smoked salmon, crème
fraîche and chives.

YOU SAY PEPPERONCINI, I say friggitello. Indeed, other names this chilli pepper answers to include the Tuscan pepper (when they are picked short, young and yellow-green) and the Sweet Italian pepper. A slightly wrinkled, classic wax-type pepper, the pepperoncino is eaten either fresh or pickled, which gives it a briny, savoury taste. A close relative is the Golden Greek pepper. In Italian and Greek cuisine the pods appear in everything from antipasti to salads, pizzas, soups and sandwiches. Not to be confused with the similarly named, but completely different spicy red peperoncini used widely in Calabrian dishes such as 'Nduja sausage, these much lower Scoville-scoring chillies have a sweet, crisp, spicy scent and a fruity taste that lifts with a slight tang.

Capsicum annuum

Chilhuacle Amarillo

SCOVILLE HEAT UNITS 100 – 500

THE TOUGH AND thin-skinned chilhuacle amarillo is a rare chilli with a sweet citrus flavour and underlying smokiness. The pendent pepper develops a rich, tangy and tart taste as it ripens from green to a deep peachy yellow. Dried, it takes on a rich, dusty golden brown colour with a mild heat and a hint of bitterness. These pods are great for stuffing, roasting or turning into a paste.

Coming from the Oaxaca region in Mexico – specifically a gorge called La Cañada where the terroir (the soil, topography and climate) is ideal – chilhuacle-type chillies are the pride of the state. In addition to the chilhuacle amarillo, they include the related apple-red chilhuacle rojo and chocolate-brown chilhuacle negro (see pages 46–47). The increased desirability of the chilhuacle negro has led to the amarillo becoming scarcer. The amarillo distinguishes itself by being elongated rather than bell-shaped like the rojo and negro. These three peppers are key in Oaxacan cooking, particularly in the region's famous *mole* sauces. Chilhuacle amarillo is the essential ingredient for the sublime and beautifully coloured *mole amarillo*, a lighter, spicier sauce than the more widely known *mole negro*, and which does not contain the dark chocolate, nuts and dried fruits usually associated with *mole*.

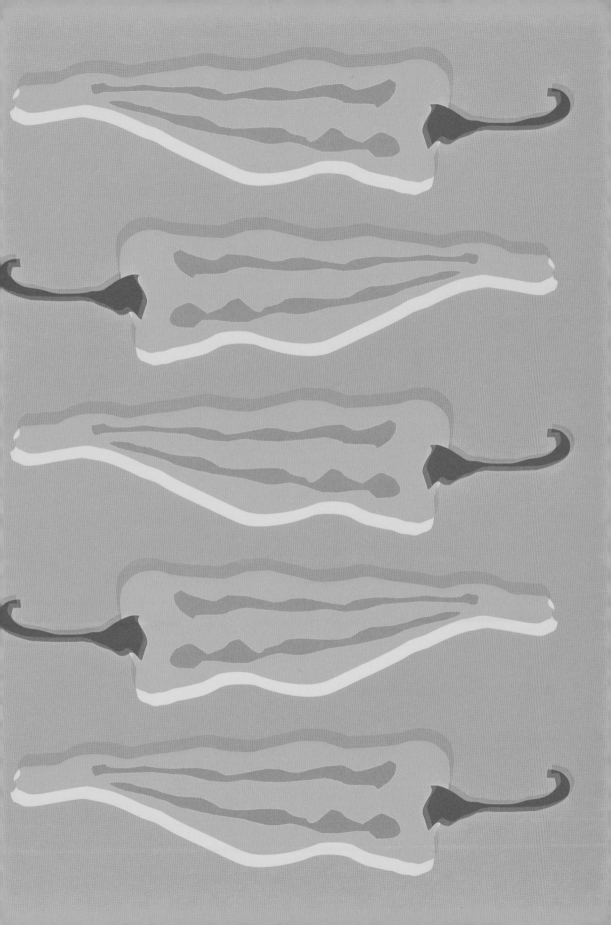

Capsicum chinense

Apricot Habanero

SCOVILLE HEAT UNITS 500 – 700

SIZE
2.5 × 6 cm (1 × 2½ in.)

ORIGIN
Dorset, UK

GROW
Simple to grow in growbags, pots or in the ground, this plant is great for beginner chilli growers and is a prolific producer of fruit.

EAT
A great chilli to share with children or anyone nervous of eating chillies. Pair with fresh apricots to make apricot habanero chutney. Delicious chopped into salads or sandwiches. Stuff with cheese, pulled pork or minced beef.

HABANERO-TYPE CHILLIES from the *Capsicum chinense* species are well known for their blistering heat but are typically avoided by nervous beginner chilli eaters. The elongated, slightly grooved and delicately coloured apricot habanero is a welcome exception as it is virtually heat-free, with a lustrous fragrance and mild, fruity taste.

Ripening from lime green to a cross between apricot orange and salmon pink, the pods are crunchy and fresh to bite, breaking open with a delicious aroma. This highly recommended pepper was bred by renowned British chilli breeders Joy and Michael Michaud at Sea Spring Farm, overlooking the English Channel in West Dorset. Joy and Michael are also the pioneers behind the Dorset Naga (see pages 200–01) – one of the hottest chilli peppers in the world – as well as many subtler, flavourful new varieties such as this one.

Researchers have established that native Brazilians brought the chilli species *Capsicum chinense* (that is, the ancestor of all habanero-type peppers) from the Amazon region to the Pacific coast of South America. Spanish colonists then brought them from Peru to Mexico and the Caribbean.

4
3
2
1
0

Capsicum annuum

Santa Fe Grande

SCOVILLE HEAT UNITS 500 – 700

SIZE
6 × 2.5 cm (2½ × 1 in.)

ORIGIN
Mexico

GROW
Easy to grow, very
productive, with large
leaves. This is a quick
grower too – it only takes
around 65 days for pods
to appear from potting.
A great chilli plant for
a balcony.

EAT
Chop into slices and add
fresh to salads or pickle
in a classic Mexican
escabeche.

THE SANTA FE GRANDE pepper is often used in its immature
pale yellow stage when it is known as a *güero* (meaning 'blond').
The pods are impressive for their colour changes, ripening from
a distinctive pale yellow to bright red, via a warm orange. With a
crunchy juiciness and only mild pungency, the Santa Fe Grande
is often eaten raw – like a mellower jalapeño – though it can also
be dried or pickled. Its slight sweetness is fresh and melon-like
and brings a bright note to everything from sauces and salads to
seasoning and sandwiches.

The Santa Fe Grande is a wax pepper pod; others include the
pepperoncini (see pages 16–17) and Hungarian Hot Wax (see pages
80–81), as well as the tiny Mississippi Sport, which is a traditional
topping for Chicago-style hot dogs in the American Midwest.

4
3
2
1
0

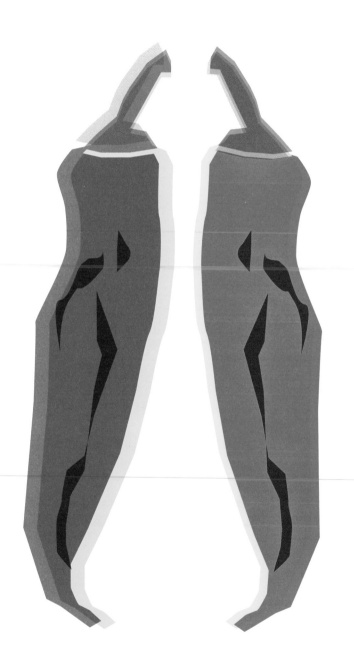

Capsicum annuum

NuMex Heritage 6-4

SCOVILLE HEAT UNITS 700 – 900

SIZE
20 × 5 cm (8 × 2 in.)

ORIGIN
New Mexico, USA

GROW
The terroir of the Hatch region makes this one best to grow there or thereabouts – though they will thrive in any uniformly warm, dry conditions with bright light.

EAT
Make *calabacitas* with chopped squash, courgettes (zucchini), sweetcorn, tomatoes and roasted green Hatch chillies. Use fresh and green in fish tacos. Use ripe and red in a rhubarb, apple and chilli chutney. Serve with margaritas using New Mexico chilli-infused tequila and lime.

THE NEW MEXICO chilli type was developed by the renowned botanist Fabian Garcia in the late nineteenth century, originally for canning purposes. Beloved across the state of New Mexico, much mythology surrounds these chillies and the town of Hatch where they are most famously grown (and therefore sometimes called Hatch Green or Hatch Red, though no such variety technically exists). The pods are delicious both unripe green and ripe red – indeed, the New Mexico state legislature adopted 'Red or green?' as the official state question (i.e., motto) in 1999. Green New Mexico chillies are eaten fresh, pickled or roasted – often in traditional clay *horno* ovens that resemble beehives. Ripened to red, which enhances their back heat, they can be dried and ground to produce chilli powder, or bunched and strung into *ristras* and hung in doorways. Sweet and crisp when fresh, with an earthy kick when dried, this versatile chilli can be used in everything from sautées and stews to guacamole and enchiladas.

The NuMex Heritage 6-4 is an upgrade of the most standard of the New Mexico chillies – the legendary New Mexico No. 6-4, which had deteriorated since its development in 1957. Paul Bosland of the Chile Pepper Institute at New Mexico State University (hence 'NuMex' in the names of chilli varieties developed there) worked with cryogenically stored seeds to produce the NuMex Heritage 6-4, which is said to have more flavour compounds than the original and higher yields.

Ají Dulce

SCOVILLE HEAT UNITS 0 – 1,000

SIZE
2 × 3 cm (¾ × 1¼ in.)

ORIGIN
Caribbean

GROW
A good container plant,
this relatively slow grower
flourishes in warm soil and
semi-shade.

EAT
Great for making mild salsas,
sauces and salads. Pair with
shrimp. Add to a round of
Bloody Marys.

A SMALL, LIGHT to dark green pepper that turns red, orange or yellow if left to mature, the ají dulce is a sweet habanero type without the intense hot lava fiery overkill. Its flavour is fruity, sweet with hints of smoke and black pepper. Especially beloved in Puerto Rico, it is sold commercially as the Puerto Rican No Burn Pepper, and also known as *ají gustoso* ('tasty pepper') or *ají cachucha* ('cap-shaped pepper') in the Dominican Republic. Ají dulce is used in Puerto Rico, Cuba and the Dominican Republic, where milder chillies are favoured, and is a common ingredient in *sofrito*, the fragrant, savoury, finely diced vegetable mix that forms the base of many Latin American dishes. It often appears in the tamale-like *hallacas* served in Venezuela at Christmas: a spiced mixture of meat, peppers, raisins, almonds, capers and olives wrapped in cornmeal dough and then steamed or boiled in plantain leaves.

Ají – pronounced *a-hee* – is a general term for chilli peppers in South America and the Caribbean. It is a Spanish version of a Taíno word meaning 'chilli' – i.e., close to what some of the original indigenous inhabitants of the Caribbean might have called their peppers. Other chillies in this book with *ají* in their names are not necessarily similar to ají dulce.

5
4
3
2
1
0

Capsicum annuum

Ñora

SCOVILLE HEAT UNITS 0 – 1,000

SIZE
2 × 3 cm (¾ × 1¼ in.)

ORIGIN
Murcia, Spain

GROW
An easy thriver in usual good chilli-growing conditions, the short, compact plants can be grown in large containers with well-drained soil. Place in direct sunlight.

EAT
Add Ñora paprika to crab cakes or mixed into mashed potato with spring onions. Celebrate the Catalan Calçotada onion festival by dunking grilled calçots (a large, mild spring onion) in a rich salsa romesco made with dried Ñoras. Try the fresh pepper sautéed or grilled with seafood, vegetables or sausage.

A PIMIENTO (that is, sweet Spanish pepper), the Ñora (also spelled Nora) is known for its mild, fruity taste. It is named for the town of La Ñora in the Murcia region of Spain, where legend has it that Christopher Columbus left his first imported New World chillies under cultivation by the local monks. With a subtle, earthy flavour, dark wine-red dried Ñora chillies are prominent in Spanish cuisine – along with the larger pimiento pepper, the choricero, which is similarly mild in heat but tangier than the Ñora. Salsa romesco, the 'Spanish ketchup' of peppers, garlic and almonds, is usually made with dried Ñora peppers and traditionally accompanies fish, vegetables or lamb. Salmorreta sauce, used to colour and flavour *arroz a banda*, is made from reconstituted Ñoras sautéed in olive oil with garlic, onions and tomatoes and ground to a paste in a pestle and mortar.

Smoked paprika is possibly the Ñora's most well known appearance in the kitchen. After harvest the peppers (Ñoras or other pimientos) are smoke-dried with oakwood and turned by hand before being milled by stone wheels, which must turn slowly as the heat from friction affects the ultimate colour and flavour of the powder. Spanish paprika comes in three varieties: sweet and mild (dulce), bittersweet medium (agridulce) and hot (picante – with added cayenne pepper).

Capsicum annuum

Beaver Dam

SIZE
12.5 × 6.2 cm (5 × 2½ in.)

ORIGIN
Hungary

GROW
Relatively easy to grow, this
sprawling, prolific producer
reaches 45 cm (18 in.) tall
with weak branches that
droop under the weight of
the pods. Provide support
if needed.

EAT
This has to be the go-to chilli
for an authentic Hungarian
goulash. Use for stuffing
or add to sandwiches.
An excellently tangy salsa
maker.

A GREAT EXAMPLE of the migratory nature of chillies, this wide-walled Hungarian heirloom vegetable-type pepper was brought to the eponymous Beaver Dam, a city in Dodge County, Wisconsin, USA, by Joe Hussli in 1912, who is also believed to have brought the Hussli Tomato pepper to the same area.

The large pods of the Beaver Dam pepper initially grow erect (that is, upside-down) on the plant before their thick, juicy flesh becomes too heavy and inevitably falls due to gravity. Horn-shaped, and starting out an electric lime-green colour, the vibrantly red ripened pods are crunchy in texture and mildly hot when seeded. They have a paprika-like slow-building heat and a versatile flavour.

So appealing is this heirloom, and at real risk of being lost, that the Slow Food Foundation for Biodiversity has listed the Beaver Dam pepper in its Ark of Taste catalogue of delicious and endangered traditional varieties.

5
4
3
2
1
0

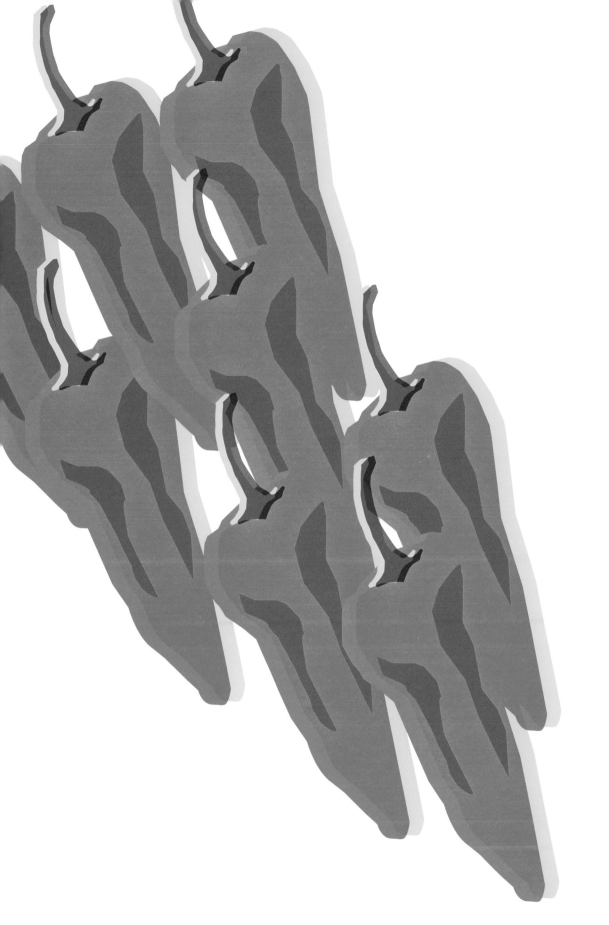

Biquinho

SCOVILLE HEAT UNITS 500 – 1,000

SIZE
1.5 × 2.5 cm (½ × 1 in.)

ORIGIN
Brazil

GROW
The bushy, highly productive plant grows up to more than 70 cm (28 in.) tall in garden beds (though pots are possible). This one will make a sensational ornamental addition to any garden.

EAT
In Brazil, the pods are commonly preserved in vinegar and served as an appetizer. They also make a fantastic jam and can perk up soups, salads, stews and sauces.

BEARING POINTED PODS shaped like raindrops, or even commas, and variously creamy white, sunshine yellow and scarlet red, the biquinho is a ravishing South American *Capsicum chinense* landrace variety. 'Landrace' means it is a domesticated plant that has been raised in a specific area for a long period of time, and has adapted to the particular conditions of the region – in this case, Brazil, where it is practically the national chilli.

In Portuguese, *biquinho* means 'little beak', which makes sense, as the pod resembles the beak of a small bird, hidden within the leaves of the plant. Alternative names are chupetinho, pimenta de bico or pimenta biquinho. The bite-size peppers have a fruity, melony sweetness and distinctive smokiness. They are often eaten pickled. Their heat is in most cases extremely modest for a *Capsicum chinense* chilli, though a few biquinho varieties (such as biquinho iracema) are significantly hotter, up to 27,000 SHU.

5
4
3
2
1
0

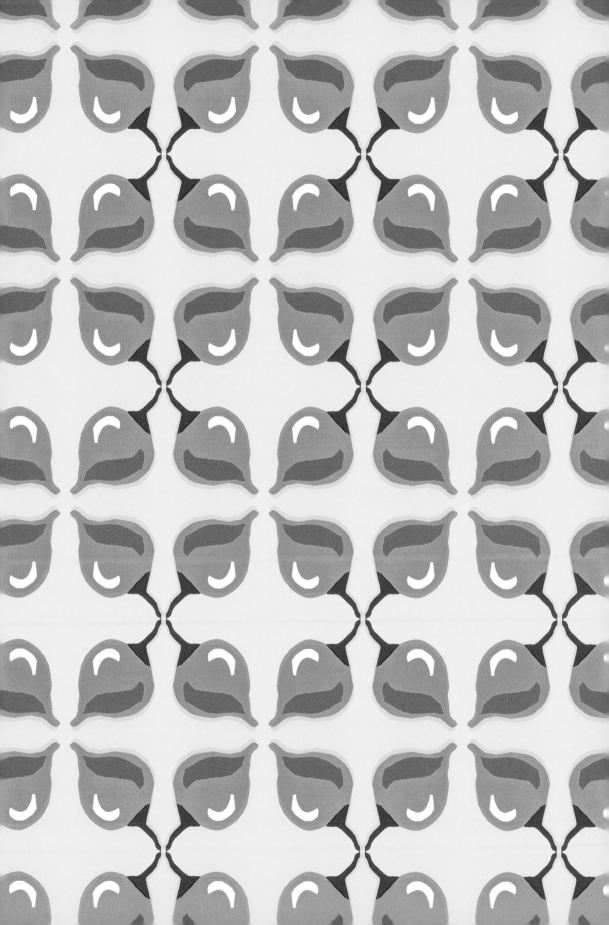

Cubanelle

SCOVILLE HEAT UNITS 500 – 1,000

SIZE
15 × 5 cm (6 × 2 in.)

ORIGIN
Italy/Cuba

GROW
The great chilli grower
(and eater) David Floyd,
writes, 'Don't grow bell
peppers, grow this instead,'
and it's an easy one to grow,
too, in lots of sun.

EAT
Fry up and use in Italian
sausage and pepper
sandwiches. Add to salads,
casseroles, soups and
sauces. Eat like a Sicilian:
bake with a pine nut and
breadcrumb stuffing.

ALSO KNOWN AS the Italian frying pepper (it is frequently found
in sausage and pepper sandwiches at Italian fairs) or the Cuban
pepper (it is very familiar in Cuban cuisine as well as in Puerto
Rico), there is a (mildly heated!) dispute over whether the pepper
actually originates in Cuba or Italy. Some call it 'the Italian
cubanelle' to get round this issue.

Only slightly hot, the walls of the cubanelle are much
thinner than bell peppers and the body shape is tapered at the end,
wavy and elongated; this pepper is all shoulder. The pods start
yellow-green and mature to a classic red colour. A similar chilli
is the banana pepper, but the cubanelle has a distinctive, sweeter
flavour and a touch more piquancy. The pepper is usually picked
at the early yellow-green stage, when it is fresh, crisp with a spicy,
simmering heat. Waiting for red pods will increase the heat level
a little.

5
4
3
2
1
0

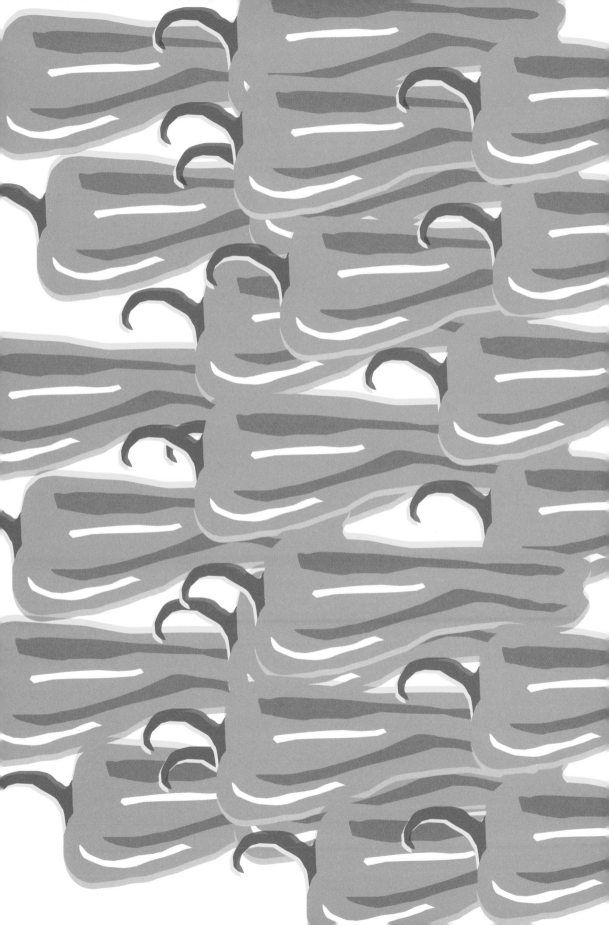

Capsicum baccatum

Peppadew® Piquanté

SCOVILLE HEAT UNITS 900 – 1,100

SIZE
2.5 × 2 cm (1 × ¾ in.)

ORIGIN
South Africa

GROW
You cannot officially buy the seeds or grow a Peppadew® Piquanté of your own. The plant was registered with the Plant Variety Protection scheme within the last 25 years and is protected.

EAT
Add to everything from omelettes, soups, stuffed peppers and kebabs to curries, salads, *spaghetti alla puttanesca*, and even desserts like vanilla mousse.

THE PEPPADEW STORY starts as every story should: on holiday. Johan Steenkamp first discovered the sweet, piquant pepper in the back garden of his holiday home in Port Elizabeth in the Eastern Cape of South Africa. The previous owner of the garden had been a botanist who travelled extensively in Central America, and it is possible that he brought the ancestors of the pepper, which is a unique variety, home from one of his expeditions to that continent. Steenkamp developed a pickling recipe for the small, vibrantly red peppers – bottles apparently exploded during its development – and set up a cottage industry, registering the brand and securing plant breeder rights. A successful buyout and a massive global marketing campaign has transformed Steenkamp's pepper into one of the chilli world's great modern commercial successes.

All Peppadew Piquanté peppers are grown in the Limpopo and Mpumalanga regions of South Africa, although Johan Steenkamp is no longer involved in their production (he still receives royalties). Resembling a cross between a cherry tomato and a small red pepper, the Peppadew Piquanté starts green, maturing to a bright orange and red, with a glossy skin and thick, juicy flesh. Sweet to the bite, they have the kick of a mild to hot chilli and are as versatile as they come (another reason for their success).

5
4
3
2
1
0

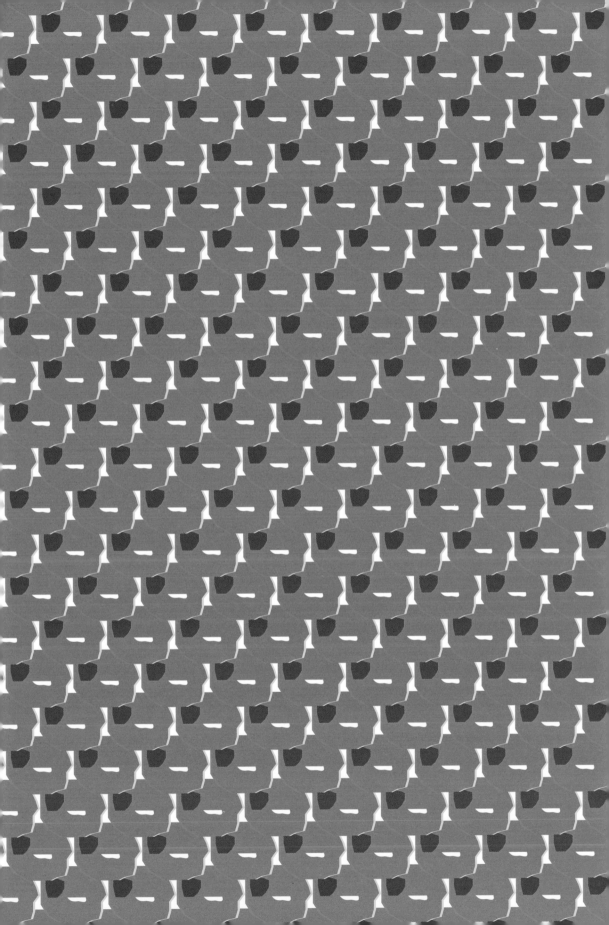

Ají Panca

SCOVILLE HEAT UNITS 1,000 – 1,500

SIZE
8 × 2.5 cm (3 × 1 in.)

ORIGIN
Peru

GROW
A prolific producer that
makes a stunning-looking
plant, growing up to 1 m
(3 ft) tall with white flowers.

EAT
Sensational in salads,
soups, salsas and sauces.
Great chopped over fish.
Use in a marinade for roast
chicken. Add it to avocado
and chocolate desserts.

ONE OF THE MOST widely used chillies in Peru (the other being the ají amarillo, see pages 142–43), and grown mainly near the coast, the ají panca is an outstanding all-round chilli pepper with a respectable heat and a crisp, curious flavour. The 'ají' in the name would normally suggest this is a *Capsicum baccatum*, like most chillies of Peruvian origin, but the white flowers on this plant make it a *Capsicum chinense*. This chilli is usually sold and eaten dried, so the pods are left on the plants to dry in the field before harvesting and further sun-drying on reed mats.

The ají panca ripens to a rich burgundy red and the dried chillies have a taste palette somewhere between berry, bean and apple, with smoky undertones. On rare occasions when enjoyed fresh, the medium thick pepper pods have a satisfying crunch; dried, they are hotter, with fresh grassy aromas. This is a great inclusive chilli with only a mild burn. It is essential in many Peruvian specialities, such as *anticuchos de corazon* – marinated beef heart threaded on wooden skewers and grilled. In Peru it is often sold as a chilli paste to be added to sauces or used as a condiment.

5
4
3
2
1
0

Georgia Flame

SCOVILLE HEAT UNITS 1,000 – 1,500

SIZE
4 × 17 cm (1¾ × 6¾ in.)

ORIGIN
Republic of Georgia

GROW
The productive plant grows up to 45 cm (18 in.) high in the semi-shade. Pods take 90 days to mature.

EAT
Try stuffing, roasting, pan-frying or drying. Use in Georgian dishes.

AN ATTRACTIVE AND PIQUANT variety from the Republic of Georgia, this bulky, thick-skinned, crunchy-fleshed pepper with wide shoulders and a tapering tip starts green and matures to an iridescent flame red. If you squint, the ripened pods might resemble licks of flame, hence the name. The pods generally bear few seeds.

The pepper has a sweet and spicy, fruity flavour: excellent in salsa or salads, it makes a great paprika or chilli jam. The fire-engine red colour of the peppers mean that, dried, they can be used as decorative chillies in *ristras* or as Christmas tree decorations.

Interestingly, Georgian dishes do not share similarities with Russian food; instead, there is a distinctive Mediterranean sensibility with plenty of fresh herbs, dried spices – and, of course, red hot chilli. Georgia Flame is a good chilli for *chakhokhbili*, a chicken stew made with tomatoes, fragrantly scented with basil, coriander, garlic, parsley, bay leaf and chilli pepper, or *ajika*, a hot, spicy paste made with hot red peppers, garlic, herbs and spices and used to flavour meat and fish dishes mainly in Samegrelo and Abkhazia.

5
4
3
2
1
0

Ancho/Poblano

SCOVILLE HEAT UNITS 1,000 – 2,000

SIZE
14 × 7 cm (5½ × 2¾ in.)

ORIGIN
Mexico

GROW
Fresh poblano plants grow best in the ground, rather than in a greenhouse. As they can reach up to 1 m (3 ft) high and produce up to 30 pods, provide stakes or strings for support.

EAT
To toast dried ancho: stem and seed the chilli before tearing into flat pieces and pressing down on a griddle or other hot surface with a spatula. Lift when you hear crackling. Toast both sides.

THIS IS THE WIDE CHILLI – *ancho* meaning 'wide'. When fresh and a dark, glossy green, it is called a poblano (meaning 'pepper from Puebla') and often served stuffed. Darker brown related varieties are called mulatos (see pages 48–49). Ancho 101 is an interesting, hotter variety, noted for its apple flavour.

Earthy, fruity, cranberry-coloured dried ancho is the most commonly encountered version of this pepper. Dried ancho can be used shredded or ground, or soaked and puréed, allowing its full depth of colour to emerge. It is most famous as an ingredient in classic, rich Mexican *mole* sauces, where the sweet, raisin-like flavour of dried ancho pairs harmoniously with bitter chocolate. Ancho is also the chilli of choice for the classic American chilli con carne (not to be confused with the rather different Mexican *carne con chile*) made famous by the 'chilli queens' of late nineteenth-century Texas, who sold plates of the stew for a dime from wagons lit up by coloured lanterns. Cocktail lovers should try smoky Ancho Reyes (infused with dried ancho pods) and its lighter cousin Ancho Reyes Verde (with green-picked poblanos) – chilli liqueurs that add spiciness, sweetness and heat to alcoholic concoctions.

Dried chillies like anchos are big business in parts of Mexico, where they are dried in hot air tunnels, or in the open air spread out on stretchers covered in straw. Once they are dried, the wrinkled chillies are flattened. Ancho is a good example of a dried chilli that reaps the rewards of toasting, which gives it complexity, char and that inimitable smokiness.

6
5
4
3
2
1
0

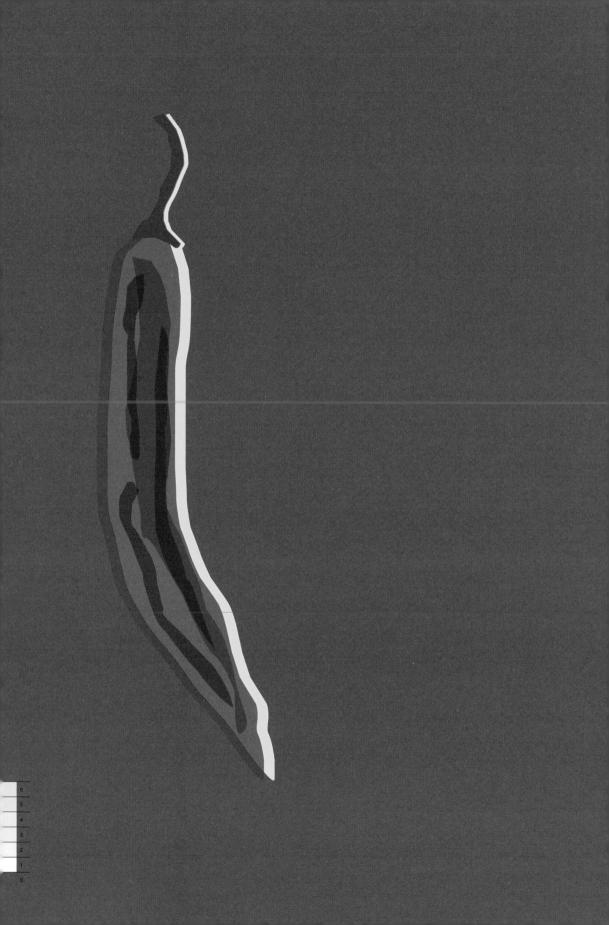

Chilaca/Pasilla

SCOVILLE HEAT UNITS 1,000 – 2,000

SIZE
15 × 3 cm (6 × 1¼ in.)

ORIGIN
Mexico

GROW
Pot-based, this vigorous plant will grow up to 1 m (3 ft) in height; significantly taller if planted in the ground.

EAT
The perfect pepper for a Mexican *mole* sauce, enchiladas, chilli con carne or salsa.

THE CHILACA PEPPER starts a dark racing green and ripens to a deep chocolatey, raisiny brown (almost black when fully matured), with a meaty, sweet flavour and only a hint of heat. The word 'chilaca' itself comes from a Nahuatl (Aztec) word meaning 'old' or 'grey hair', a reference perhaps to the wrinkled, twisted quality of the pods that somehow seem to suggest the wisdom and appearance of old age. Fresh chilaca peppers, though rarely sold outside Mexico, make a delicious green salsa or can be used in similar fashion to the more commonly encountered serrano (see pages 104–05).

The chilaca is mostly found dried, in which state it is called a pasilla, meaning 'little raisin' in Spanish, referring to both the rich, sweet, earthy aroma and the dark brown colour of the dried pod (though not, clearly, to this chilli's relatively large size). The pasilla is hotter than the fresh chilaca and is frequently used in Mexican soups, and in sauces such as *adobo* and *mole*. Ground, it makes a good all-purpose chilli powder and can be substituted for dried ancho, with which the pasilla is sometimes confused, occasionally even on packaging labels. The slightly hotter smoke-dried Pasilla de Oaxaca has a chipotle-like taste; the darker Pátzcuaro variety grown in Michoacán traditionally flavours local dishes such as *sopa tarasca*, a pinto bean soup.

Chilhuacle Negro

SCOVILLE HEAT UNITS 1,000 – 2,000

SIZE
5 × 10 cm (2 × 4 in.)

ORIGIN
Oaxaca, Mexico

GROW
Although seeds are available outside Mexico, this one really has to be grown in Oaxaca to develop its flavour, but it is still a beautiful and interesting plant to try in any gardening climate.

EAT
If you are lucky enough to have chilhuacle negro peppers, making a *mole negro* is the only sensible thing to do with them.

CHILHUACLE NEGRO IS the caviar of chillies, one of the three chilhuacle varieties ('huacle' comes from the Nahuatl word for 'dried') that are native to a gorge in Oaxaca State in Mexico called La Cañada, unique for its terroir. In danger of extinction, the chilhuacle negro is the most expensive chilli pepper in the world: 500 g of a premium negro will set you back about $150 (£120).

Like its sisters – the similarly shaped but red chilhuacle rojo, and the lighter, longer chilhuacle amarillo (see pages 18–19) – the negro features in the much celebrated Oaxacan *mole* sauces. The *mole negro* made with chilhuacle negro – try Diana Kennedy's recipe for *mole negro oaxaqueño* in her classic *Oaxaca Al Gusto: An Infinite Gastronomy* – is one of the most rarefied chilli experiences going. And it *is* going: chef and culinary historian Maricel E. Presilla recounts in detail how the northern Oaxacan indigenous groups growing and drying chilhuacles for market are dwindling and ageing, to the point there are only five left. The rarity of this famous chilli has led to the market being flooded with inferior-quality versions.

The bell-shaped chilhuacle negro, with its deep black sheen, is often reserved for special occasions – and rightly so. The pod has a complex flavour profile with the sweetness of dried fruit, tobacco and cocoa, the subtlety of artichoke, and the freshness of bell pepper. The pepper will usually be dried before a paste is made from it for a dark, thick, sweet and spicy *mole negro*.

Mulato Isleño

SCOVILLE HEAT UNITS 1,000 – 2,000

SIZE
8 × 15 cm (3 × 6 in.)

ORIGIN
Puebla, Mexico

GROW
These big plants – 1 m
(3 ft) high – grow best in
the ground, or in a pot with
support as the large pods
gain weight.

EAT
Roast for green poblano
soup. Stuff with meat or
cheese for a genuine *chile
rellenos poblanos*. Make a
mole poblano. Add to ice
cream and chocolate cake
recipes. Pair with raspberries
and blood oranges.

POBLANO TYPES ORIGINALLY came from the state of Puebla in Mexico and are a crucial element in Mexican cooking. This poblano type (see also ancho, pages 42–43) is an heirloom pepper that builds slender heart-shaped walls, making for a sweeter, meatier, deeper flavour with overtones of liquorice and oak. Dried naturally, the mulato isleño takes on raisiny, molasses notes and can be rehydrated with water before being blended into sauces.

Starting a deep, glossy green – when they are normally picked and prepared in Mexico – the pepper pods ripen to a rich, dark chocolate-red. They are versatile chillies, perfect in everything from stuffed starters to *mole* sauces and rich desserts. *Chiles en nogada* is an artful patriotic Mexican dish that involves poblano-type chillies like mulato isleño filled with *picadillo* (a blend of shredded meat, fruit and spices) and topped with a walnut-based creamy sauce and pomegranate seeds – making the green, white and red colours of the Mexican flag.

6
5
4
3
2
1
0

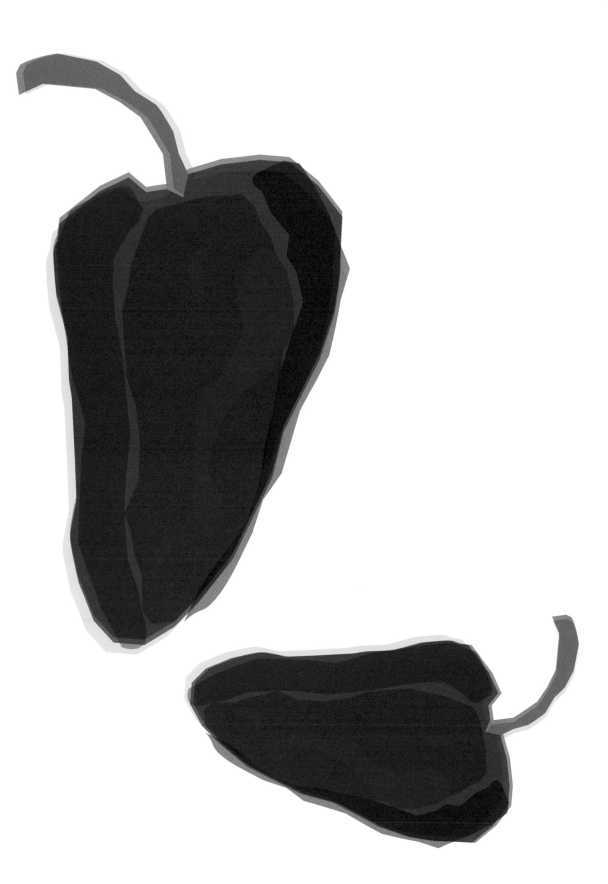

Kashmiri Mirch

SCOVILLE HEAT UNITS 1,500 – 2,000

SIZE
5 × 2.5 cm (2 × 1 in.)

ORIGIN
Kashmir, India

GROW
The bushy plants can grow to about 85 cm (35 in.) and a greenhouse is certainly recommended in cooler climates.

EAT
Add Kashmiri Mirch chilli powder to any Indian dish; sprinkle over beans or cheese on toast for garnish and a subtle kick. Make a sweet potato and spinach curry and season with Kashmiri Mirch powder for colour before serving.

NATIVE TO THE northernmost state of India, this famously bright crimson-coloured, smooth and shiny chilli pepper is in much demand for Indian cuisine, imparting its intense colour more than its mild heat. Kashmiri Mirch peppers are usually dried and ground into a powder (sometimes also called *deghi* or *deggi mirch*). The powder will redden anything that can absorb colour (think oils, fats, onions, meats) and so if you are looking for a substitute for Kashmiri Mirch the point is to go for a colourful powder like paprika rather than a hot one like ground cayenne. With its subtle, sweet and fruity taste as well as colourful hue, Kashmiri Mirch is used in recipes for tandoori (clay oven) preparations, *rogan josh* and the curry sauces that accompany Kashmiri *biryani*. Other important Indian chillies include the similar but much spicier Byadagi chilli, grown in Karnataka; the ubiquitous green, finger-like pusa jwala (see pages 140–41); and of course bhut jolokia (see pages 204–05) and the Nagas, some of the hottest chillies in the world (see pages 200–03).

Make your own Kashmiri Mirch powder: halve 6 chillies before throwing in a medium-hot cast-iron pan. Toast for 5 minutes, then cool completely before blending to a powder in a spice grinder. Keep in an airtight jar.

6
5
4
3
2
1
0

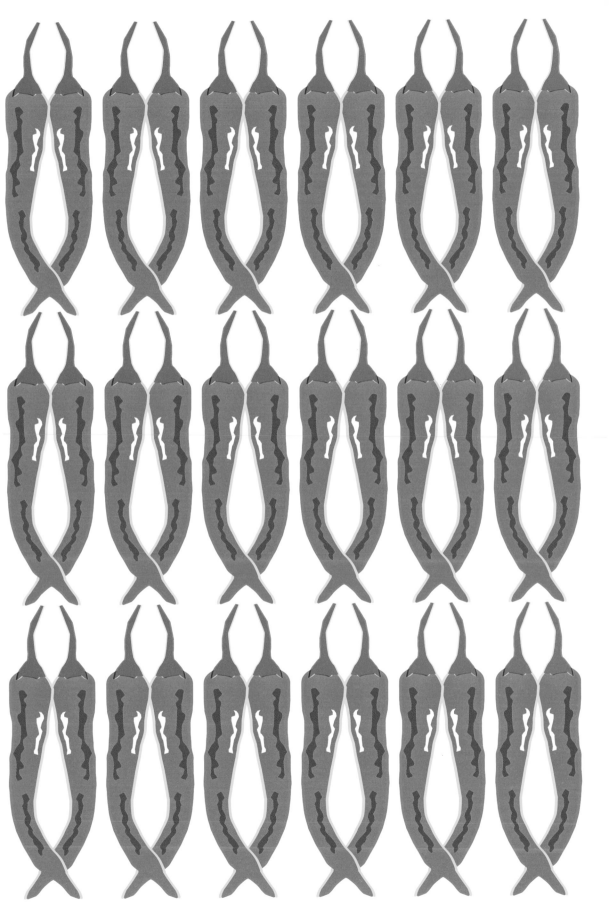

Capsicum annuum

Anaheim

SCOVILLE HEAT UNITS 500 – 2,500

SIZE
3 × 15 cm (1¼ × 6 in.)

ORIGIN
California, USA

GROW
Plant in rich soil to grow big pods and keep the soil moist. Good for containers, but grows up to 60 cm (2 ft) tall, so provide some form of support.

EAT
Stuff for *chiles rellenos*: roast or char the pepper, then fill with a melting cheese like Monterey Jack, dip in egg batter and deep-fry. Or fire-roast and cut into strips, before adding to soups. Add fresh to salads and stir-fries, or pickle.

A GREAT, MILDLY HOT chilli pepper, the elongated and shiny dark lime-green Anaheim was originally grown by Emilio C. Ortega in 1894. An entrepreneurial resident of Anaheim, California (the Orange County city is also known for its theme parks, including Disneyland), Ortega travelled to Mexico, bringing back some chilli pepper seeds with him. He pioneered a method that involved roasting, peeling, seeding, washing and preserving his green Anaheim pods in jars (which later became cans). To this day, the Ortega company still sells its original fire-roasted green chillies, 'America's favourite!'

When green, the skin is tough and needs peeling off: roast on an open fire, barbecue, or griddle pan until the skins are burnt; when cool, peel away flesh (keeping some for the special burnt taste). If left to ripen purplish-red, the Anaheim is called a Chilli Colorado or California Red and will shrink considerably in size and lose moisture; they are sweeter then too. In dried form, it becomes a seco del norte, one of the mellowest red chillies available.

6
5
4
3
2
1
0

Capsicum annuum

Cascabel

SCOVILLE HEAT UNITS 1,000 – 2,500

SIZE
3 × 2 cm (1¼ × ¾ in.)

ORIGIN
Central Mexico

GROW
Recommended for both outdoor and greenhouse growing, the cascabel is easy for a beginner and has good yields.

EAT
Use fresh in casseroles, soups, sauces and salsas. Use dried in the classic Mexican dish *menudo* (tripe soup). Make a purée by steeping dry-fried cascabels in just-boiled water for 15 minutes before blending to a smooth paste, and combine with grapefruit and orange juice for a marinade.

SOMETIMES CALLED A chile bola (Spanish for 'ball chilli'), jingle bell, or rattle chilli (the loose seeds make a rattling sound when the dried pod is shaken), the round and red cascabel chilli is spherical and not unlike a cherry pepper (see pages 58–59) in appearance, though with a thinner skin. The name cascabel itself means 'little bell' or 'sleigh bell' in Spanish and the resemblance is certainly there. This chilli is often confused with the similarly named – but different – cascabella chilli.

Cascabel's flavour is woody with nutty undertones and a slight astringency. The mild to moderate heat has a pleasing warmth, rather than a fiery burn, and so this chilli is perfect for sauces and it pairs well with fruit. The cascabel is often used dried, when the skin turns a deep red-brown colour; flaked, the dried cascabel can be added to soups and stews or roasted tomatoes. In Mexico the chilli is used in *birria*, a hearty goat, beef or chicken stew made with cinnamon, cloves and cumin and served in the mornings; it is reputedly a hangover remedy.

6
5
4
3
2
1
0

Rocotillo

SCOVILLE HEAT UNITS 1,500 – 2,500

SIZE
4 × 5 cm (1½ × 2 in.)

ORIGIN
Peru

GROW
Sow early and grow in warm sun. Rocotillo plants grow up to more than 1.2 m (4 ft) tall and develop a bushy canopy with crinkly leaves. Prolific producers, the pods mature from green to red over 150 days.

EAT
Make salsas with fruity rocotillo. Good for pickling. Sprinkle lime juice, dried rocotillo flakes and a few sea salt flakes on ripe mangoes.

WITH ITS RESEMBLANCE to the pattypan squash in shape, the little wrinkled rocotillo is sometimes also known as the squash pepper. The rocotillo is a beloved chilli of the West Indies and Puerto Rico, with a pleasantly mild heat (though admittedly underwhelming to chilliheads). A quick note on identity: there are rocotillos of similar taste and appearance from both the species *Capsicum chinense* and *Capsicum baccatum*. (*Capsicum baccatum* originated in Peru and is one of the smaller chilli groups, including many of the famous South American ají peppers, such as ají amarillo, see pages 142–43.) The rocotillo should not be confused with ají rocoto, a similarly named but much hotter Peruvian pepper, also known as manzano, from the species *Capsicum pubescens* (see pages 116–17).

Ripening to orangey yellow or luscious red, this beautifully perfumed pepper is rounded and squat with furrows, tapering to a point. Rocotillo pods are thinly fleshed and taste fresh and fruity (pair them with mango in a salsa). The chillies are regularly used in Caribbean soups, stews and sautéed vegetables, or for dressing beans; they accompany a shrimp rice pilaf well. The rocotillo is a staple of jerk meat (chicken and pork) dishes. With its thin walls, this chilli dries successfully: at which point chop into sauces and salads.

6
5
4
3
2
1
0

Capsicum annuum

Cherry

SCOVILLE HEAT UNITS 0 – 3,500

SIZE
3 × 3 cm (1¼ × 1¼ in.)

ORIGIN
Mexico

GROW
A good garden grower, and as ornamental as it is useful. The smooth leaves are dark green and the flower corollas are white.

EAT
Add chopped fresh cherry peppers to salsas, salads and sautéed or roasted vegetables. Cook down to make jams and chutneys. Pair with goat's cheese and prosciutto.

NAMED FOR ITS RESEMBLANCE to cherry fruits in size and shape, the cherry pepper was mentioned in botanical literature as early as 1586 and illustrated in Basilius Besler's *Hortus Eystettensis*, a Bavarian herbal published in 1613. Originally from Mexico, the plant was introduced into England via the West Indies in the mid 1700s. Variations include the cherry chocolate, the cherry sweet, the cherry bomb (a particularly hot one) and the heirloom variety called Besler's Cherry.

When fresh, these globe-like peppers – sometimes with a blunt point – are orange to bright red. The walls are thickly fleshed, which makes the cherry perfect for pickling since it absorbs the brine well. These are also good peppers for stuffing; for instance, roasted and filled with goat's cheese as canapés. The pods are either borne upright or hang pendent if on the larger side. They are fruity in flavour and though their heat is normally mild, some hotter versions exist.

Capsicum annuum

Berbere Coffee Brown

SCOVILLE HEAT UNITS 1,000 – 5,000

SIZE
10 × 2 cm (4 × ¾ in.)

ORIGIN
Ethiopia

GROW
The plant grows well in
pots, with white flowers,
reaching a height of 60 cm
(2 ft). It does well in cooler
climates.

EAT
The fresh pods make a great
coffee-brown chilli sauce.
Dry and grind for a hot
Ethiopian chilli powder.

THE WIDE PENDENT PODS of this rare Ethiopian heirloom variety start green and slowly turn a reddish chestnut brown: the more sun that reaches them, the redder they will be. With tasting notes of dark herbal sweetness, a hint of chocolate, and a fruity, smoky tang, this is a fascinating chilli for any collection. The crunchy walls are thin and firm; the pods are juicy with an upper to middling heat that builds and a pleasant accompanying burn.

Drying adds complexity to the flavour and so this pepper works well as a chilli powder for sauces and stews, especially Ethiopian dishes such as beef *wat*. 'Berbere' refers to the classic Ethiopian spice mixture comprising ground chillies, korarima, rue, basic, garlic, ginger, ajwain, fenugreek, nigella, cardamom and clove.

7

6

5

4

3

2

1

0

Capsicum annuum

Cyklon

SCOVILLE HEAT UNITS 1,000 – 5,000

SIZE
3.5 × 11 cm (1½ × 4½ in.)

ORIGIN
Poland

GROW
A fairly low-maintenance chilli, the 75 cm (30 in.) plant with white flowers may need support during growing.

EAT
Make your own cyklon paprika. Ferment in a hot pepper sauce. Chop and add fresh pods to stir-fries and salsas.

PEPPERS FOUND THEIR WAY to Poland after the conquistadors brought them back to Spain from Mexico and the Ottoman Turks planted them in Hungary, which they occupied during the sixteenth and seventeenth centuries. The cyklon is a dark red heirloom Polish pepper with long, tapered, slightly curved fruits and a gentle warmth. The pod's thin flesh makes it good for drying, so the Polish spice industry uses it primarily to make paprika – a word that, incidentally, comes from the Polish *pierprzyca*, even though it was the Hungarians who perfected the spice to season their goulash. So gentle is the pepper's warmth that Poles even call it the 'half-hot' pepper. Its formal name is Polish for 'cyclone' (which, meteorologically speaking, Poland lacks as much as this pod lacks heat). Maturing from emerald green to a deep red, cyklon pods are also used fresh in salsas and salads, with a heat that fades quickly. Poland's national dish *bigos*, a stew of slow-cooked meat, sausage, sauerkraut, mushrooms and other vegetables, can be seasoned with cyklon paprika for extra authenticity.

7
6
5
4
3
2
1
0

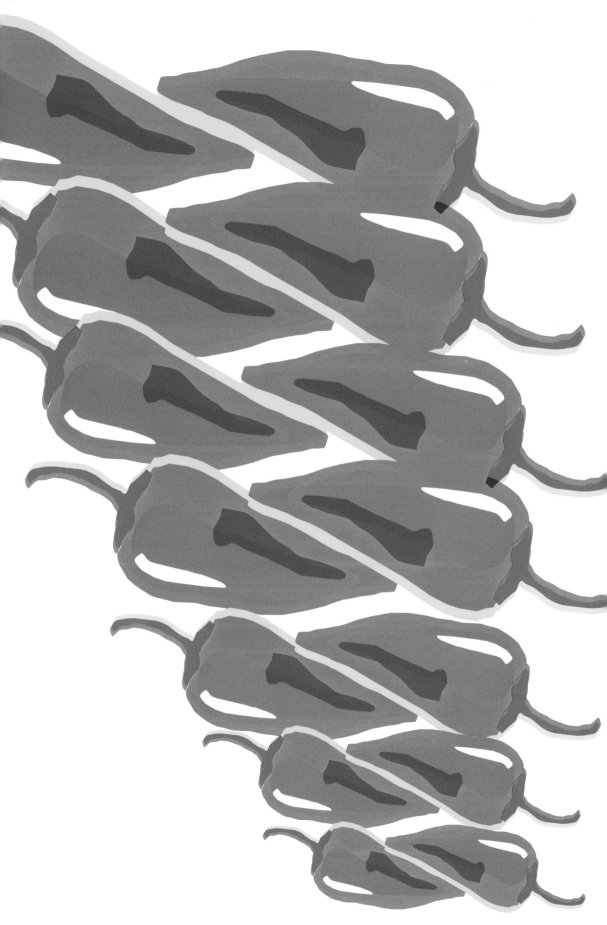

Guajillo

SCOVILLE HEAT UNITS 2,500 – 5,000

SIZE
13 x 4 cm (5 x 1½ in.)

ORIGIN
Mexico

GROW
In good sun and moist soil,
the plants grow up to 60 cm
(2 ft), producing around 50
pods per plant.

EAT
Add dried whole or
shredded pods to tortilla
soup (also known as *sopa
Azteca*). Make a guajillo
paste with garlic and
oregano as a marinade
for meat. Use to make the
North African condiment
harissa and stir into pilafs
and stews.

ONE OF THE MOST commonly used dried chillies in Mexico, long, rich orange-burgundy red, glossy, conical guajillo chillies have a moderate heat and fruity taste. Guajillos are the dried form of the fresh green mirasol chilli pepper (see also NuMex Mirasol, pages 66–67; pulla, pages 76–77). Most guajillo peppers hail from the dry climate of north central Mexico; those grown in Peru and China are hotter, and considered less desirable. Because the seeds in the dried guajillo pods rattle a little, this chilli is sometimes confused with the differently shaped cascabel (see pages 54–55).

This is a good all-rounder for dried use, and features in many Mexican *moles*, salsas and braised dishes; it can also be ground for chilli flakes or powder. Dried guajillo sometimes also lends its earthy, fruity heat well to Mexican hot chocolate made with milk. The chilli's flavour has bright, tangy notes of tannin, charred wood and green tea.

7
6
5
4
3
2
1
0

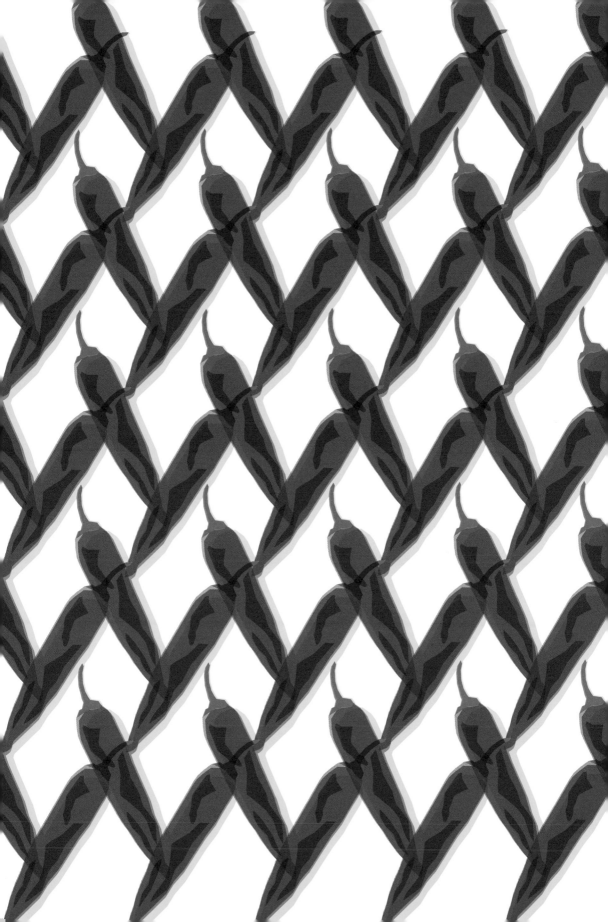

Capsicum annuum

NuMex Mirasol

SCOVILLE HEAT UNITS 2,500 – 5,000

SIZE
2 × 5 cm (¾ × 2 in.)

ORIGIN
New Mexico, USA

GROW
The average plant grows up to 60 cm (2 ft), with white flowers and pods in attractive clusters.

EAT
Use fresh in salads or dry for turning into a powder, and add to soups, sauces and stews.

THE NAME OF the Mexican mirasol pepper means 'looking at the sun' in Spanish – reflecting the fact that the fruits grow erect on the plant, with their tips pointing upward. Dried mirasol peppers are known as guajillos (see pages 64–65) and a staple of Mexican cooking; fresh mirasol peppers, with their fruity, mild taste, are especially popular in Peruvian cuisine.

The NuMex Mirasol – with its smooth texture, shiny surface and brilliant red pods – is a rather different mirasol-type chilli, developed primarily as an ornamental at New Mexico State University in 1994 by Paul Bosland and Max Gonzalez. Their aim was to create an attractive pepper pod for incorporating in decorative wreaths or in flower arrangements. The thin-walled fruits are pungent and green when immature and turn red with maturity, with a bitter note to the flavour. The pods can, however, be eaten if desired: use fresh in salads or dried and ground to a powder for cooking.

7
6
5
4
3
2
1
0

Brown Egg

SCOVILLE HEAT UNITS 3,000 – 5,000

SIZE
5 × 3 cm (2 × 1¼ in.)

ORIGIN
Unknown, possibly Europe

GROW
A rather rare, robust and bushy plant that heads up to 1 m (3 ft) with a protruding crown.

EAT
Stuff and grill, or pair with Mexican *huevos revueltos*: scrambled eggs with tomatoes and onion and served with avocado and fresh coriander (cilantro).

THE PLUMP, EGG-SHAPED pods start a rich green before ripening to a deep chocolate brown, with thick walls and a smoky habanero flavour. The pods are juicy with an intense fruitiness and their satisfying ovoid shape makes them particularly good for stuffing and barbecuing or grilling. There is a question mark over the SHU scale of this one – reports vary and it has been noted as high as 80,000 SHU, though most have a much gentler heat, with an aromatic, spicy quality. We found ours through the fantastically named Hippy Seed Company run by Neil and Charlotte Smith in Australia. They sell hard-to-find chilli seeds from around the world, but – unusually – did not have origin details for this one. If you do get your hands on a Brown Egg, they recommend it 'freshly chopped and sprinkled over your dish or stuffed with cream cheese and grilled on the barbecue'.

7
6
5
4
3
2
1
0

Capsicum annuum

Piment d'Espelette

SCOVILLE HEAT UNITS 3,000 – 6,000

SIZE
10 × 3.5 cm (4 × 1½ in.)

ORIGIN
Espelette, France

GROW
This one is growable, of course, but what makes the Piment d'Espelette is the terroir of the region.

EAT
Use in chicken *basquaise* with chorizo. Make jams, paste, and sauces. Infuse oil and sea salt. Enhance sausages and pâtés. Pair with chocolate.

THIS ONE IS A REAL reminder of the power chilli has to bring people together and help forge ritual and community. The Espelette Festival was founded in 1967 and is still very much going strong. Each year Espelette – with its quirky half-timbered Labourd houses – hosts the celebration of the pepper harvest with ten other villages in the Pyrénées-Atlantiques region of France. The chillies are strung into garland *ristras* that festoon the streets and houses (anything with a hook gets one) and thousands of spectators flock to see the festival procession in traditional dress, accompanying a service of thanksgiving and initiations to the brotherhood of Piment d'Espelette. The culmination of the festival is a gigantic banquet of Espelette-inspired dishes: the elongated red chilli is particularly famous for its role in curing Bayonne hams, as well as being crucial in other classic Basque dishes such as green pepper *pipérade*, fish stew and chicken *basquaise*. The pepper itself is mostly used as a dried, sweet, smoky powder – a Basque-specific paprika.

Chillies aficionado David Floyd notes that the pepper was introduced to the region in 1523 by a Basque navigator, Gonzalo Percaztegi, who travelled with Christopher Columbus on his second American voyage. So important is this chilli to the region that it has been granted Appellation d'Origine Contrôlée status in France, and EU Protected Designation of Origin.

11
10
9
8
7
6
5
4
3
2
1
0

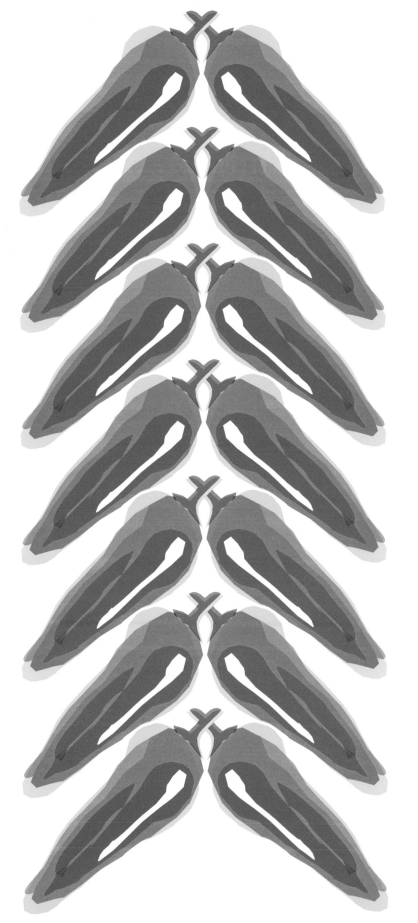

Capsicum annuum

Chimayó

SCOVILLE HEAT UNITS 4,000 – 6,000

SIZE
10 × 3 cm (4 × 1¼ in.)

ORIGIN
New Mexico, USA

GROW
Easy to grow, though –
as with Champagne grapes
– if the plants are not reared
in the specific climate
and soil conditions that
make the Chimayó region
special, you will get only
an approximate imitation.

EAT
Roast, use dried or flaked,
or sprinkle dried Chimayó
powder, called *Chimayó
molido*, over meat, fish
and vegetables.

NAMED AFTER ITS New Mexico hometown, just 50 km (30 miles) north of Santa Fe, the Chimayó heirloom pepper (a local landrace) has been revived thanks to the hard work of a non-profit group called the Chimayó Chile Farmers.

The peppers grow in the Chimayó foothills near the snowcapped Sangre de Cristo mountains, irrigated by a mountain stream – unique climatic, environmental and geological conditions that give the pepper its special qualities (in wine terms, the terroir). This is 'sacred dirt', after all – the local soil has long been credited with miraculous powers of healing, and Chimayó has been a pilgrimage site since the nineteenth century.

The result is a sundried pepper pod with twists and knots that offers a smokier, earthier taste than other New Mexico peppers. Under the not uninteresting heat, there is a lingering citrus tang, depth and richness that is unique to the Chimayó.

11
10
9
8
7
6
5
4
3
2
1
0

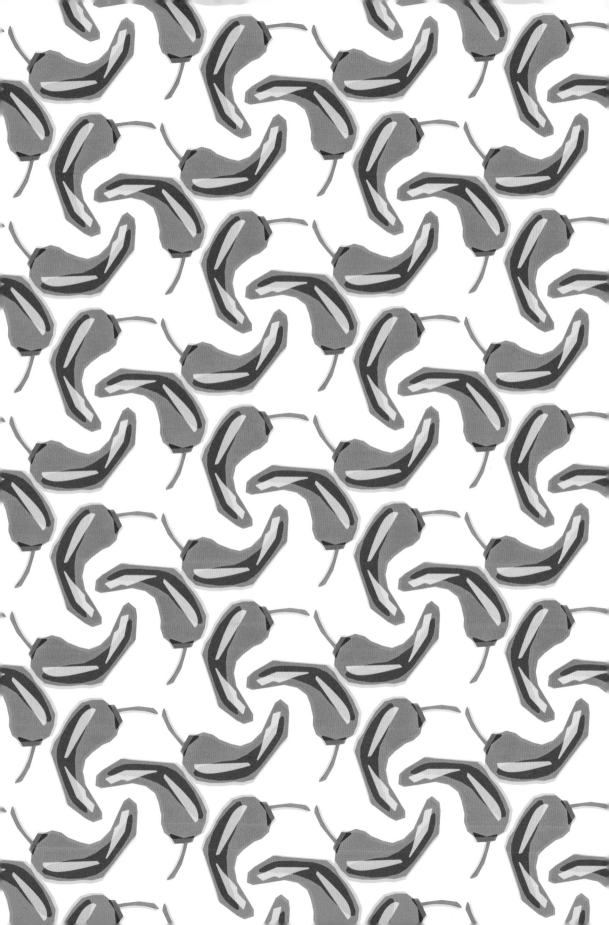

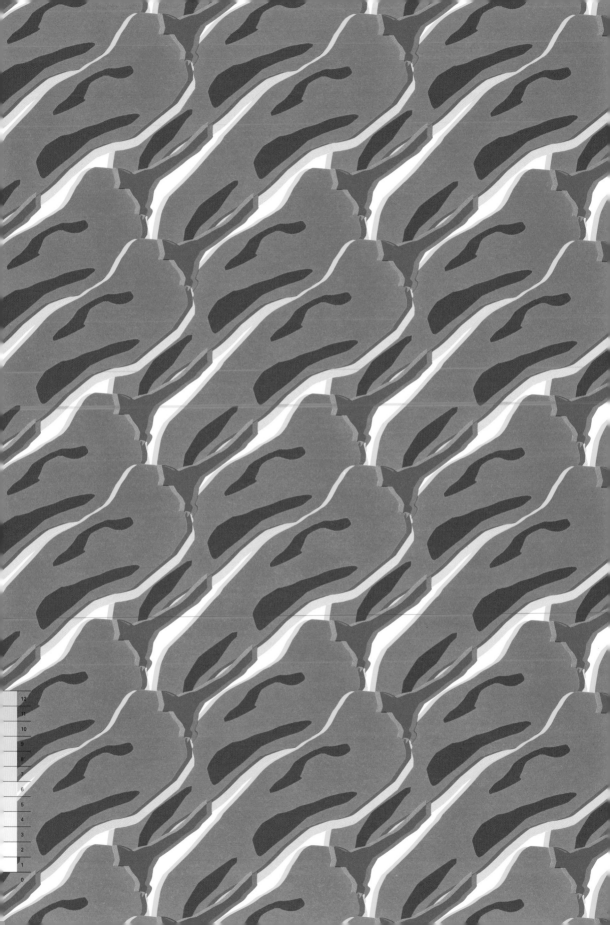

Capsicum annuum

Sandia

SCOVILLE HEAT UNITS 2,000 – 7,000

SIZE
12 × 3 cm (4¾ × 1¼ in.)

ORIGIN
New Mexico, USA

GROW
Relatively easy to cultivate, upright plants head to 60 cm (2 ft) under good chilli-growing conditions.

EAT
A good all-rounder for dried use. Grind to make a top-quality chilli powder. Inspired by British food journalist Joanna Blythman, add sandia chilli flakes and chopped anchovies to purple-sprouting broccoli sautéed in butter and oil.

A NEW MEXICO TYPE chilli developed in the 1950s at New Mexico State University and originally a cross between the New Mexico No. 9 and Anaheim, the sandia has thinner walls and more heat than the NuMex Heritage 6-4 (see pages 24–25). The additional mild fruity sweetness that surfaces after the warmth is also part of the sandia's charm, and makes a superb chilli powder. Ageing from a classic green pepper colour to a rich red, the sandia tapers with a slight curve, making this a simultaneously functional and ornamental pepper for the garden. It is also a good pepper to dry for *ristras*, wreaths and other decorative purposes.

The sandia was primarily intended to be used red-ripened and dried, as chilli powder or chilli flakes – its thin walls make it easier to dry than other New Mexico peppers. On the rare occasions fresh pods are available outside New Mexico, they can also be roasted and used for salsas. The Sandia Select variety, on the other hand, has thicker walls and was developed for green chilli use – with the same heat levels as the ordinary sandia, it is a spicier alternative to milder green New Mexico chillies such as Anaheim (see pages 52–53).

Capsicum annuum

Pulla

SCOVILLE HEAT UNITS 2,000 – 8,000

SIZE
8 × 3 cm (3 × 1¼ in.)

ORIGIN
Mexico

GROW
These sturdy plants are prolific. The bushy pulla plant can grow up to 75 cm (30 in.) high and the long pods are usually used dried, so only pick when fully matured.

EAT
Excellent in *moles* and salsas that call for fruity and spicy sweetness, this chilli goes particularly well with chicken and fish. To maximize flavour, roast for 3–4 minutes on a high heat or in a dry griddle pan.

ANOTHER OF THE Mexican mirasol peppers (see page 66), the reddish-brown dried pulla (sometimes spelled 'puya') has a superb, fruity flavour with berry and liquorice undertones and a dry heat. It is sweeter and has twice as much of a kick compared to the related guajillo (see pages 64–65). The elongated pod has a curved, tapering tip and is smaller than the guajillo. When dried it turns from an orangey red to a metallic translucent dark maroon with a shiny surface.

Mostly used dried and ground to a powder, pulla, like guajillo, is a good chilli for puréeing into sauces, casseroles, marinades, chutneys, stews and soups. Pulla peppers are sometimes used in sangrita, the traditional Mexican non-alcoholic tequila chaser – a blend of pomegranate juice, grenadine and pulla chilli powder (though recipes vary by region).

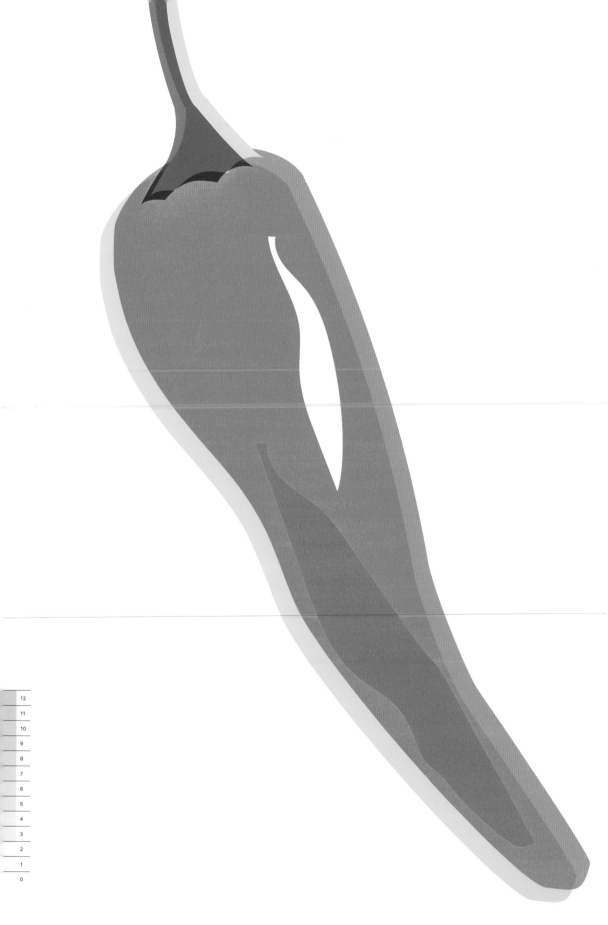

Capsicum annuum

Bulgarian Carrot

SCOVILLE HEAT UNITS 2,000 – 8,000

SIZE
2.5 × 10 cm (1 × 4 in.)

ORIGIN
Hungary/Bulgaria

GROW
The chunky, quick-ripening plant grows to 1 m (3 ft) high and produces plenty of pods. This plant does well in colder climates, though as with most chillies it enjoys plenty of sun.

EAT
Make Bulgarian Carrot jelly or hot sauce. Mix in a salsa with pineapple or mango. Cut up into stir-fries. Make a chilli salad with carrot, beetroot, mint, ginger and a honey citrus dressing.

IF EVER THERE WERE a quintessential Cold War chilli, it is the heirloom Bulgarian Carrot, also known as shipkas, allegedly smuggled out from behind the Iron Curtain in the 1980s and a popular ornamental and culinary pepper ever since.

This charming carrot lookalike, with its bright orange pointedness, starts green, then turns yellow before ripening to an impressive, almost fluorescent, carrot-orange. The pepper pods are normally picked and eaten only when fully ripe.

Spicy, crunchy, fruity, sweet and fresh to taste, the thin-skinned shipkas is typically used in salsas and chutneys but can also be roasted or pickled.

Capsicum annuum

Hungarian Hot Wax

SCOVILLE HEAT UNITS 2,000 – 8,000

SIZE
20 × 5 cm (8 × 2 in.)

ORIGIN
Turkey/Hungary

GROW
Ideal for cool climates: sow in early spring, nipping off any prematurely early fruit to help the plant to grow. At the end of the season, pull the whole plant up (before the frost) and hang it by the roots indoors, picking pods when needed.

EAT
Great for stuffing with cheese or beef. Or just grill, barbecue or fry. Pickle. Make sweet chilli jam. Chop into salads, salsas or sandwiches.

THIS HOT AND WAXY Hungarian is not too hot and its waxiness is more a glossy sheen. Trade descriptions aside (it is also sometimes called the yellow hot wax pepper), this is an excellently versatile chilli pod that grows on a compact, bushy 1 m (3 ft) high plant. The long, pointed, fleshy pods begin a pale yellow colour – it is unsurprisingly also known as the hot banana – before ripening to orange and then red. The redder the hotter, as (almost) ever, though this pod is often picked when it is light green and apple-like in flavour.

Supposedly brought to Hungary by the Turks in the sixteenth century, this chilli's sweet, fruity flavour made it a hit in kitchens; it is best fresh, and can be used like a spicier version of the bell pepper. The warm, lingering heat on this chilli will leave your lips burning, but it is more than bearable, and can be chopped into salads and stir-fries or stuffed with minced beef or goat's cheese and herbs.

12
11
10
9
8
7
6
5
4
3
2
1
0

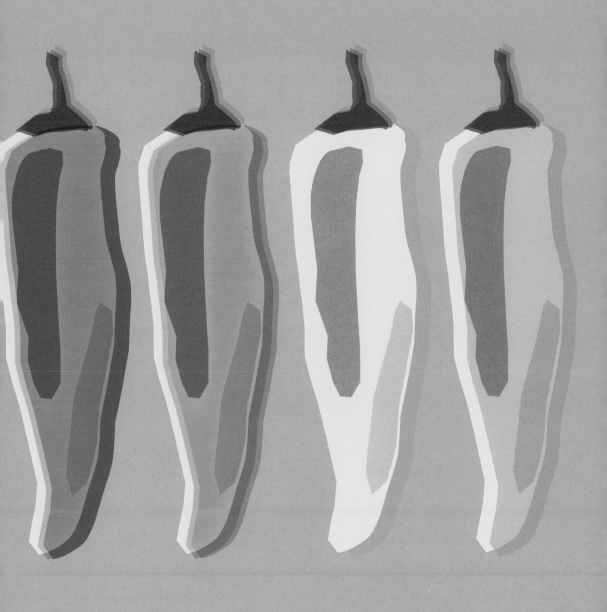

Capsicum annuum

NuMex Primavera

SCOVILLE HEAT UNITS 7,500 – 8,500

SIZE
5 x 2.5 cm (2 x 1 in.)

ORIGIN
New Mexico, USA

GROW
A compact, bushy plant
that can grow up to 90 cm
(36 in.) with a 45 cm (18 in.)
spread. It will do well in
containers.

EAT
Great for stuffing, roasting
or smoking. Turn into salsa.
Pickle.

A THICK-WALLED, jalapeño-shaped pepper with round shoulders
and a broad rounded tip, the pods of the NuMex Primavera offer
the flavour of the familiar jalapeño (see pages 90–91), minus the
fulsomeness of heat. Indeed, this cultivar was deliberately developed
by Paul Bosland and Eric Votava at New Mexico State University to
provide a mild jalapeño option for the American palate, particularly
for the stuffed, breaded and fried whole jalapeños popular as
appetizers. The skin of the pods does not tend to show the net-like
scarring, known as corking, characteristic of standard jalapeños.
(Corking is considered a desirable chilli trait in Mexico but less so
in the USA.) Gardeners find this plant favourable: easy to grow,
pleasant on the eye, and with a mild pungency.

12
11
10
9
8
7
6
5
4
3
2
1
0

Spaghetti

————

SCOVILLE HEAT UNITS 8,500

SIZE
30 × 0.7 cm (12 × ¼ in.)

ORIGIN
Dorset, UK

GROW
The spaghetti chilli pepper plant grows tall, up to 1 m (3 ft), and top heavy – so be ready to provide support. Grow these late maturers in larger pots.

EAT
It would be highly appropriate to match dried spaghetti chilli with tomatoes and garlic in a simple sauce poured over freshly made spaghetti.

A CURIOUSLY DISTINCTIVE British chilli variety, developed by Joy and Michael Michaud at Sea Spring Seeds in Dorset, the spaghetti chilli plant yields copious, long, extremely thin pods that loosely resemble its pasta namesake.

With wrinkled skin and a sharp point, the pods are relatively mild in heat, and their thin skin makes them easy to dry – indeed, the fruit of the spaghetti chilli are so long and thin that the tips often start drying before the stalk end is fully ripe. Especially good for drying, spaghetti chillies make great Christmas chilli wreaths and *ristras*. Dried, they are also easily ground into a homemade paprika.

There are competitions at some British chilli festivals to see who can grow the longest chilli. Pods of the spaghetti chilli have been known to grow to 40 cm (16 in.) so this plant would be a good contender for the crown.

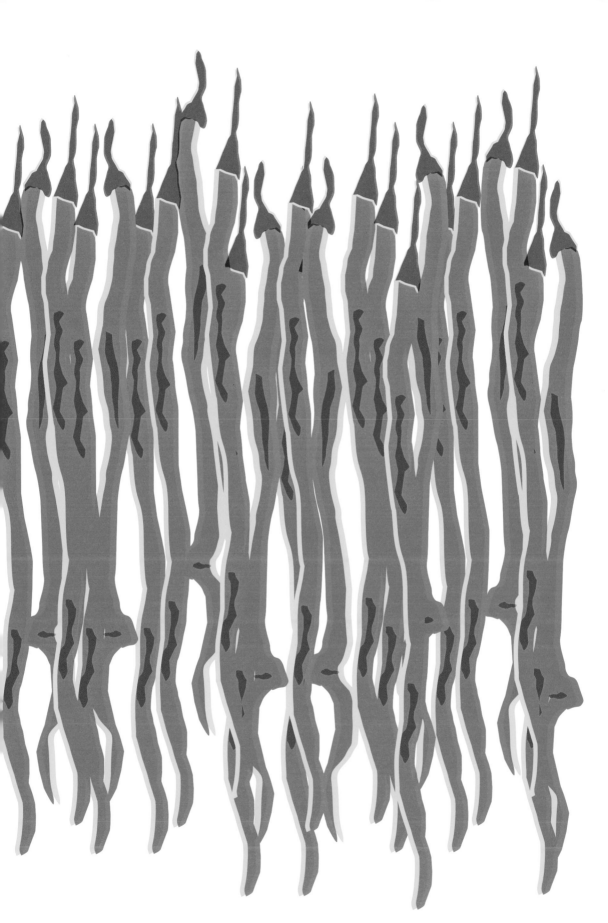

Capsicum annuum

Hangjiao 8 Total Eclipse

SCOVILLE HEAT UNITS 1,000 – 10,000 (it has not been tested)

SIZE
25 × 4 cm (10 × 1½ in.)

ORIGIN
China/Outer Space

GROW
The hard work of sending the seeds into space has already be done. This intergalactic pepper now happily grows up to over 70 cm (28 in.) in an ordinary earth-bound pot.

EAT
A very versatile chilli pepper if you can get your hands on one: good for stuffing, roasting and mild chilli sauces.

IN PURSUIT OF A SOLUTION to feeding China's growing population, scientist Jiang Xingcun discovered in the 1980s that sending vegetable seeds into space increased mutation rates by hundreds of times, speeding up the process of selecting and breeding plants for beneficial new features, such as higher yield. Chilli seeds were included in these experiments. Hangjiao means 'space pepper' – other Chinese chillies derived this way include the Hangjiao 7 Super Nova and the Hangjiao 9 Big Bang.

A short trip into the cosmos randomly alters the genetic makeup of seeds by exposing them to radiation and zero-gravity, and some of those that return show improvements in size, taste, nutritional value or disease resistance. Selected seeds like Hangjiao 8 Total Eclipse subsequently undertake a five-year programme of cultivation and field-testing until those with the best properties are ready for market.

The Hangjiao 8 Total Eclipse tastes much like an Anaheim chilli (see pages 52–53), although it is slightly hotter. The pod shapes vary from elongated to contorted corkscrew. Very sweet and juicy, it is a good all-rounder, ready for chopping into salads, stuffing, or turning into vibrant salsas.

16
15
14
13
12
11
10
9
8
7
6
5
4
3
2
1
0

Capsicum annuum

Fresno

SCOVILLE HEAT UNITS 2,500 – 10,000

SIZE
6 × 2 cm (2½ × ¾ in.)

ORIGIN
California, USA

GROW
Growing up to 45 cm (18 in.),
the Fresno needs all any
chilli plant needs: lots of full
sun and well-drained soil.

EAT
Great in *pico de gallo* salsa,
ceviche, hot fermented
sauces, marinades, soups
and salads. Use as a
substitute for jalapeño.
An excellent roaster.

THE WIDE, PLUMP, thumb-sized Fresno pepper is the dependable lookalike brother of the jalapeño (see pages 90–91). The Fresno is wider than the jalapeño and has thinner walls (so the jalapeño is better for stuffing; the Fresno for chopping into salsa) and offers a smokier, fruitier, tarter taste. Sold green, the Fresno pepper is milder in heat (2,500–10,000 SHU, as above); the riper red version gets a lot hotter than a jalapeño, more like a serrano (see pages 104–05). This is a chilli best used pickled or fresh, rather than dried and ground.

Despite their brotherly appearance, the Fresno pepper is not related to the jalapeño, but is a New Mexico-type chilli developed in the early 1950s by Californian farmer Clarence Brown Hamlin, whose self-taught experiments in trying to find 'a different flavour' eventually led to the variety he named after his local city of Fresno ('ash tree' in Spanish). Today, Fresno peppers are grown throughout California, especially in the San Joaquin Valley.

Capsicum annuum

Jalapeño/Chipotle

SCOVILLE HEAT UNITS 3,000 – 10,000

SIZE
3 × 10 cm (1¼ × 4 in.)

ORIGIN
Mexico

GROW
The plant rises up to 1 m (3 ft) in height. They are easy to grow, though they prefer full sunlight.

EAT
Use fresh jalapeños to make salsa, serve chopped over nachos, or purée and add to chilli avocado soup. Make a fermented Sriracha-style sauce with red jalapeños. For roasted chipotle nuts, toss cashews, walnuts, almonds and pecans with oil, lime juice, brown sugar, salt, chipotle powder and chopped fresh rosemary; roast *c.* 20 minutes until golden.

THE JALAPEÑO IS NAMED after the Mexican town of Xalapa (or Jalapa), where this popular thick-walled chilli was originally sold (though it may have originated in surrounding regions), and there is evidence that it was sold in Aztec markets. Conical or nearly cylindrical in shape, the dark green jalapeño pod matures to a bright red. Its skin often displays brown net-like scars called corking, which indicates higher heat levels and is considered especially desirable in some countries. Some jalapeño cultivars, such as the tamed jalapeño and the NuMex Primavera (see pages 82–83), are mild; others are significantly hotter.

Red-ripened, dried and smoked, the jalapeño becomes a chipotle. Due to their high moisture content, the pods are difficult to sun-dry so are slowly desiccated over fires of fruit woods such as apple, hickory or pecan, imparting the chipotle's famously smoky flavour. Whole, dried chipotles can be added straight to slow-cooked stews or rehydrated in a little hot water for 15 minutes, then chopped and used in salsas and other dishes for a smoky note. Chipotles are also frequently sold pickled and canned in vinegary red *adobo* sauce that is delicious as a steak sauce or marinade – or even, in Oaxaca, on *chapulines* (fried or roasted grasshoppers, a traditional snack).

16
15
14
13
12
11
10
9
8
7
6
5
4
3
2
1
0

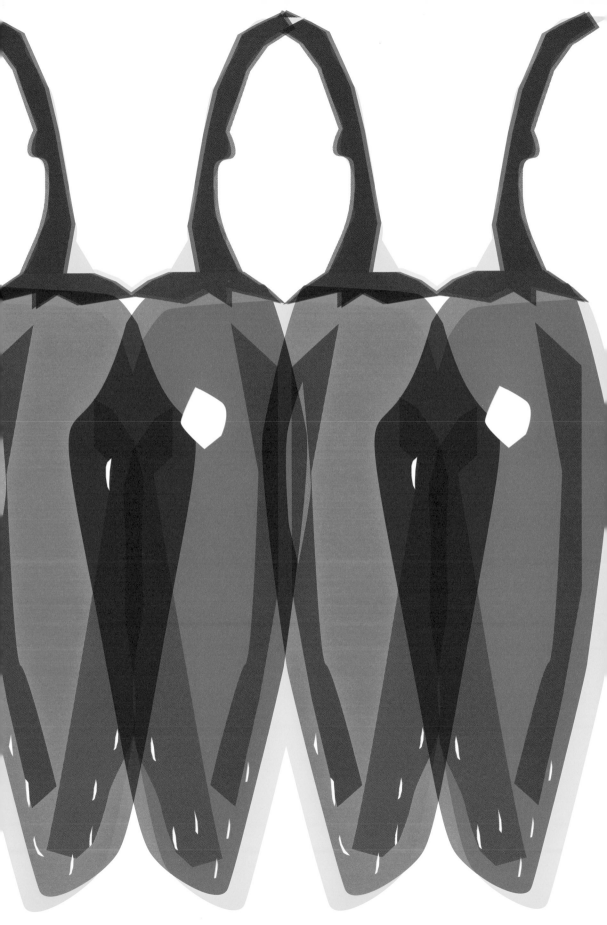

Capsicum annuum

Pimientos de Padrón

SCOVILLE HEAT UNITS 0 – 12,000

SIZE
4 × 2 cm (1½ × ¾ in.)

ORIGIN
Galicia, Spain

GROW
Germination requires warm temperatures of 18–22°C (65–72°F). The plant grows to 50 cm (20 in.) high. This is a prolific pod producer through to the middle of autumn.

EAT
Generally just eaten blistered and salted, on their own. Yotam Ottolenghi serves his with rosemary, thyme, garlic and red wine vinegar. If you encounter a mature, red pod, stuff with cheese and bake.

THE TOWN OF PADRÓN, in the Galicia region of north-western Spain, is famous for these little fried green peppers with their delicate herbal notes of asparagus and grass. The thin-skinned peppers, seemingly, were brought over by missionaries from South America in the 1500s and grown in the *huerta* (vegetable garden) of the Franciscan monastery of San Antonio de Padua in neighbouring Herbón, which hosts the annual Pimientos de Padrón festival in August.

These petite pimientos are sometimes called Russian Roulettes: each bite of one is a gamble given that one in ten have a wild heat (the rest are as placid as bell peppers, although this feature is not unique to Padrón pods – all chilli varieties have their very hot and very mild outliers). The pods are picked young and green when no longer than 4 cm (1½ in.) – leaving them on the plant will end up with much hotter, 10 cm (4 in.) pods. Japanese shishito peppers are a similar type of pod (just slightly longer) and can be substituted for Pimientos de Padrón.

Preparing Pimientos de Padrón for an effortlessly elegant hors d'oeuvre is simple: fry on a hot, heavy cast-iron pan with a light coating of olive oil until they char, then sprinkle with sea salt and serve warm. The result is an intensely peppery, pungent flavour with a sweet heat. For the authentic touch, serve with a dry fino sherry or Galician pear cider.

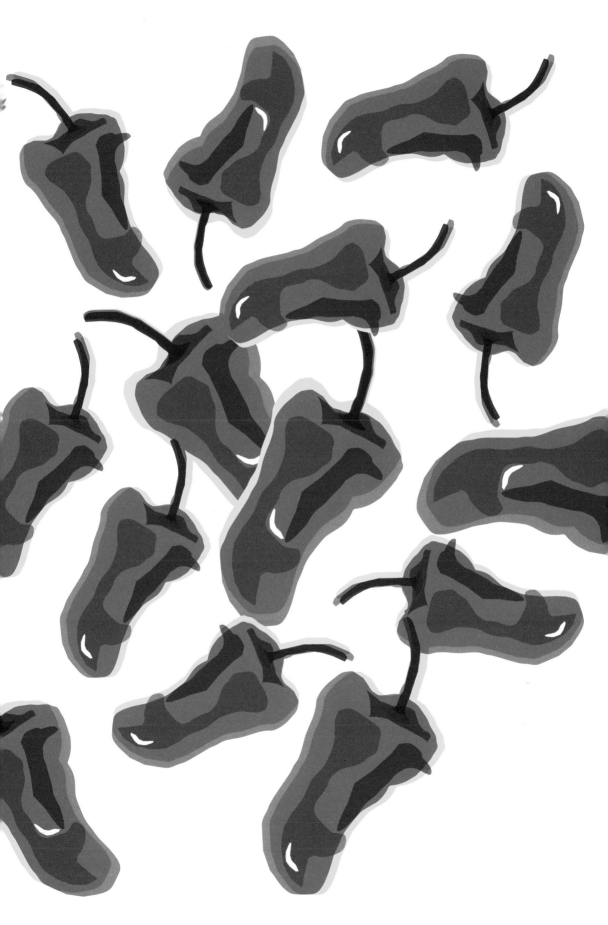

Costeño

SCOVILLE HEAT UNITS 2,000 – 12,000

SIZE
7 × 2 cm (2¾ × ¾ in.)

ORIGIN
Mexico

GROW
A low-maintenance chilli
that will grow well in good,
sunny conditions.

EAT
Good in all kinds of soups,
sauces and stews, salads
and stir-fries. Pair with garlic
and tomato.

ONE TO EAT by the seaside: the costeño pepper – its name means 'coastal' in Spanish – is related to the guajillo, one of the most commonly grown in Mexico. Also known as chile bandeño ('the banks of the river'), the costeño rojo and the milder, related costeño amarillo are from the regions of Guerrero and Oaxaca, respectively. The costeño rojo matures from green to red-orange with a conical or elongated shape. The thin-walled pods have an apricot-like, grassy flavour and a modest heat that lingers. The costeño amarillo is shinier and amber-gold in colour, with a gentler heat and a fresh citrus flavour with similarly grassy undertones. Both peppers' thin walls make them easy to dry, which is how they are usually sold.

In Mexican cuisine, the costeño rojo is used in red *mole costeño*, which traditionally accompanies chicken (or iguana), and in *mole de olla*, a rich soup with beef, corn, green beans and *xoconostle* (a cactus fruit) that is popular in central Mexican states. The understated heat and flavour of the costeño amarillo makes it blend well with a whole host of vegetables and meat; it features in several southern Mexican sauces, including *mole amarillo*.

Jean Andrews, the famed Texan author, botanist, artist and cook known as the 'Pepper Lady', recounts a rather exciting chilli whodunnit involving the costeño amarillo: 'I was called upon to identify some peppers which were considered as evidence of some sort in a double murder case in west Texas. I determined the yellow costeño from southern Mexico to be the pepper found at the scene of the crime. It was not, however, the murder weapon.'

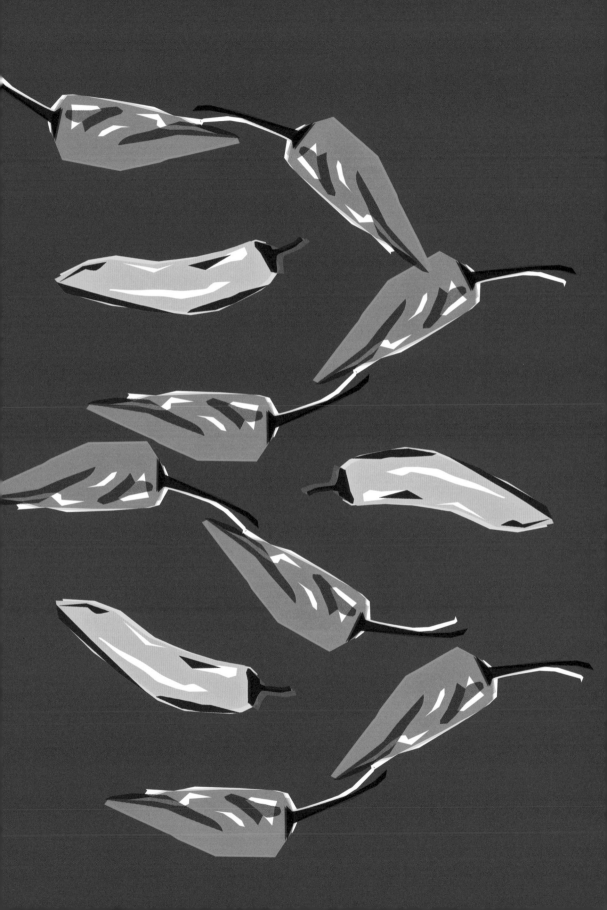

Capsicum annuum

Aleppo Pepper

SCOVILLE HEAT UNITS 8,000 – 12,000

SIZE
10 × 3 cm (4 × 1¼ in.)

ORIGIN
Syria

GROW
These plants can grow up
to 1.2 m (4 ft) tall in full sun
with moderate watering.
They are frost-tender, so
wait until risk of freezing
nights has passed before
planting out.

EAT
Make the classic Levantine
dip *muhammara* with Aleppo
flakes, red peppers, walnuts
and pomegranate molasses.

A BRIGHT RED CHILLI with a pointed end, the Aleppo pepper
(also known as the Halaby pepper) is traditionally grown in gardens
in the north of the Syrian city, once on the Silk Road and famous
as one of the oldest cities in the world, more recently as the site
of a prolonged, destructive siege during the Syrian Civil War.
Chillies drying on balconies and terraces were a familiar sight in
Aleppo before the siege. Given the difficulty of growing the pepper
during wartime – farming families had to abandon their fields due
to the threat of violence – the Aleppo pepper is now listed on Slow
Food Foundation's Ark of Taste list of rare and at-risk foods, and
has started to be grown in the USA and elsewhere.

Important in Syrian cuisine, the dried chilli is generally used
in flake form or crushed and mixed with olive oil and salt, seasoning
soups, meats, salads, pasta dishes and vegetables. It has a robust,
fruity flavour, with a hint of cumin that tickles the back of the throat.

Buena Mulata

SCOVILLE HEAT UNITS 5,000 – 20,000

SIZE
10 x 1.5 cm (4 × ½ in.)

ORIGIN
North America

GROW
A very special chilli plant to grow on a summer terrace and adaptable to most kinds of cultivation.

EAT
Perfect in salsa morada with green peppers, sugar, salt, unsweetened chocolate powder and fresh coriander (cilantro).

THIS IS AN HEIRLOOM treasure for which we are thankful to Horace Pippin, the African American folk artist who gave the seeds – probably from his friends in black catering communities of Philadelphia and Baltimore – to American food writer William Woys Weaver's grandfather in exchange for bee-sting therapy. Weaver found a jar of the seeds buried in a deep freezer in his grandparents' basement a decade after his grandfather's death and grew a few plants from the thawed seeds. He wrote about the beautiful colours of the pods – maturing from violet to pink, orange, brown and eventually deep red – and later passed them around heirloom seed-sharing groups.

Long, pointed, violet-coloured and cayenne-like, this exceptionally beautiful chilli pepper has an equally exceptional heat. Weaver suggests the name buena mulata (meaning 'the merry mulata') comes from a 1920s Cuban hot sauce whose label depicted a biracial woman (for whom *mulatta* is now considered an offensive term). Although it resembles a commercial pepper called Aurora, the buena mulata is said to be better flavoured – and much older.

Heirloom chillies like this are precious. As seed saver Owen Taylor of the Philadelphia Seed Exchange writes: 'heirlooms only survive if someone removes them from storage and places them in soil; and stories only live when they are told.'

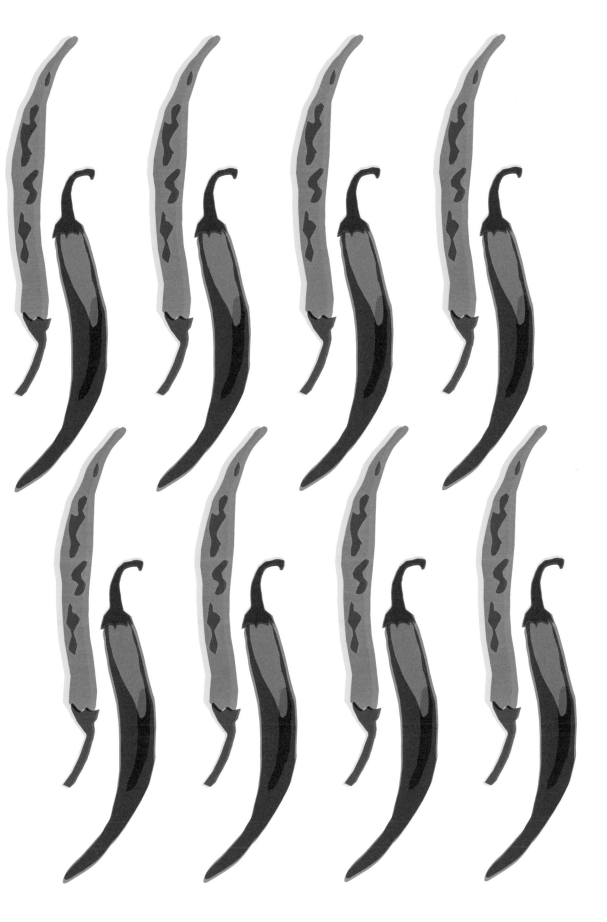

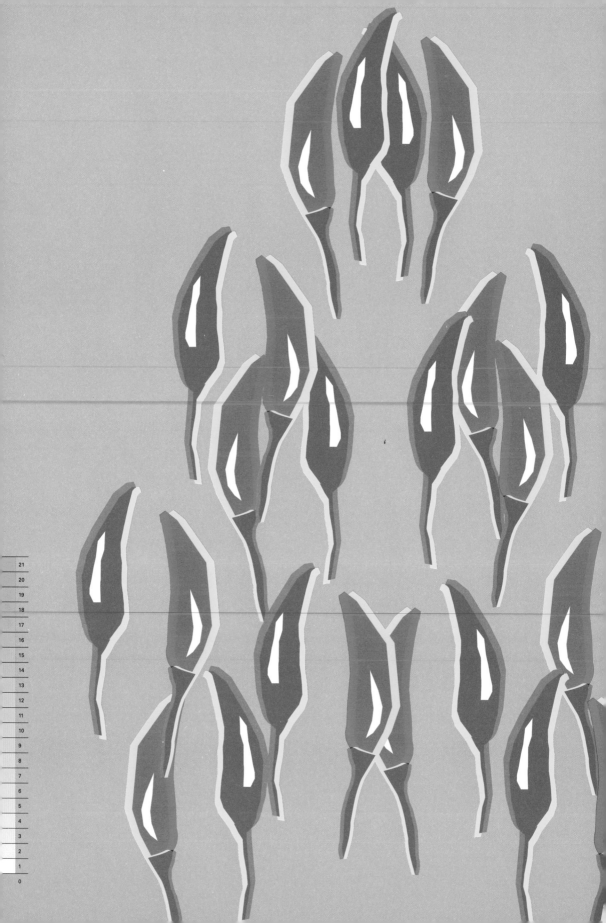

Capsicum annuum

Cheongyang Gochu

SCOVILLE HEAT UNITS 5,000 – 20,000

SIZE
2 x 8 cm (¾ x 3 in.)

ORIGIN
South Korea

GROW
The plant grows up to
1 m (3 ft) high. The seeds
require warm temperatures
for germination, 20–30°C
(68–85°F).

EAT
A versatile chilli: use green
in stir-fries, soups, pickles,
or – for the very brave – raw
and dipped in salt, soy sauce
or *gochujang*.

CHILLIES ARE MUCH LOVED in Korea, where they are called
gochu. Some are used fully ripe and dried, as chilli flakes (*gochugaru*)
or as a chilli-flavoured fermented bean paste called *gochujang*
that flavours everything from soups and stews to pan-fried pork.
The South Korean national dish *bibimbap* – a bowl of warm white
rice served with vegetables, beansprouts, egg and sliced meat – is
usually topped with *gochujang*. *Kimchi* – Korean pickled vegetables –
involves cabbage or daikon (a type of Japanese radish) mixed with
hot chillies, fresh garlic and ginger, sugar, soy sauce, and herbs.

Cheongyang Gochu – named for the rural Cheongyang
County region from where it is said to originate – is one of the
hottest and most famous chillies used in South Korea. It has a
tangy taste and a warming heat, which varies considerably, though
normally around 10,000 SHU when picked green and used fresh,
often in soups. Red-ripened and dried, it is much hotter, and makes
a mean chilli flake for seasoning *kimchi* and spicy sauces.

Capsicum annuum

Loco

SCOVILLE HEAT UNITS 24,000

SIZE
2.5 × 1 cm (1 × ⅓ in.)

ORIGIN
UK

GROW
These neat, compact
ornamental plants have
a cascading habit and are
ideal for growing in larger
pots. Support is unlikely
to be necessary.

EAT
Great for adding to salsas,
hot salad dressings and chilli
con carne.

LOCO IS A BEAUTIFUL, high-yielding ornamental chilli plant
developed by British firm Vegetalis, who specialise in 'creative
vegetable breeding', including 'patio edibles'. This variety is an
easy picker and a tasty grower. The little pods explode with a crazy,
intense heat, and delight the eyes with their colourful transformation
as they mature from lilac purple to orange and red. The plant's
purple-fringed white flowers and dark green leaves also help make
this one a beautiful addition to the garden before fruiting even starts.
And given the heat – which is not insignificant – Loco is a valuable
addition to any chilli grower's repertoire, providing both beauty
and utility. Growing upright above the attractive foliage, the pods
resemble LED lights, and brighten up salads, salsas and sauces with
glimmers of spice and colour.

Capsicum annuum

Serrano

_____

SCOVILLE HEAT UNITS   10,000 – 25,000

SIZE
2 × 7 cm (¾ × 2¾ in.)

ORIGIN
Puebla and Hildago, Mexico

GROW
Sow a couple of seeds per pot in late winter, leaving indoors in a consistently warm place. The serrano grows up to 60 cm (2 ft) tall (taller if planted in the ground) producing up to 50 pods per plant.

EAT
Make a *pico de gallo* (literally, 'beak of the rooster'): chop together serranos, tomatoes, onion and a large bunch of fresh coriander (cilantro), mix with lime juice and salt, and serve with tacos. Pickle with carrots and onions. Bake in scones.

CLIMB EVERY MOUNTAIN (and the Scoville scale). Originating from the Sierra mountains of the Mexican states of Puebla and Hildago (*serrano* means 'from the mountains', a name the chilli shares with the Spanish ham), the small, finger-shaped serrano chilli peppers have thin, smooth skins, dark green to scarlet when ripe, and juicy, thick, almost kiwi-like flesh inside. The fleshiness means this is not a chilli for drying.

The torpedo-shaped serrano has a 'pure-and-simple' heat according to Mexican food writer Rick Bayless; it certainly hits quickly with a fresh, intense, upfront burn at the back of the throat and a pungent, slow-building flavour. This well-seeded tongue stinger has lasting apple-ish, grassy notes and a distinctive bitterness. Varieties include the purple serrano and the serrano tampiqueño, which is particularly hot. The serrano is classically used in the salsa *pico de gallo* and gives a fresh, biting heat chopped into guacamole. *Aguachile* is a Mexican ceviche in which fresh raw prawns are 'cooked' in a thin, acidic marinade made with serrano chillies, lime juice, red onion and cucumber.

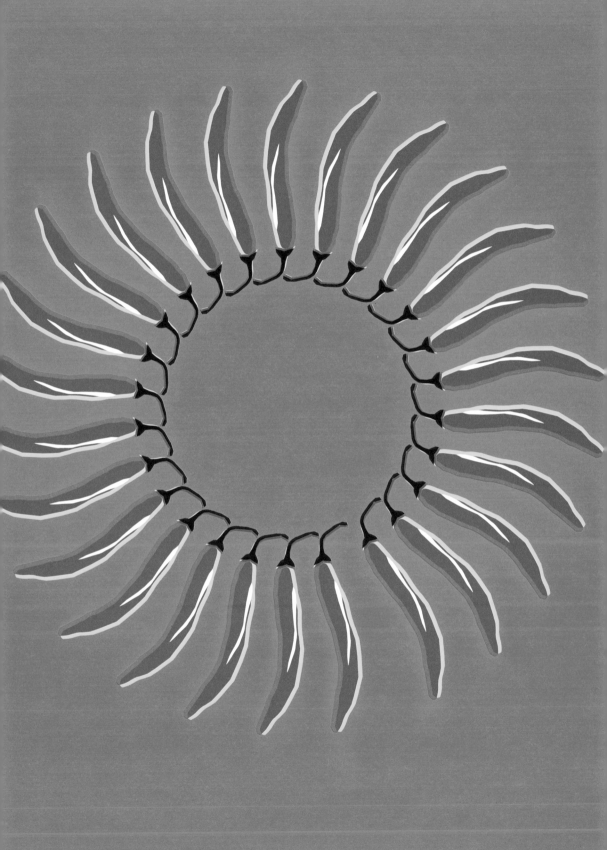

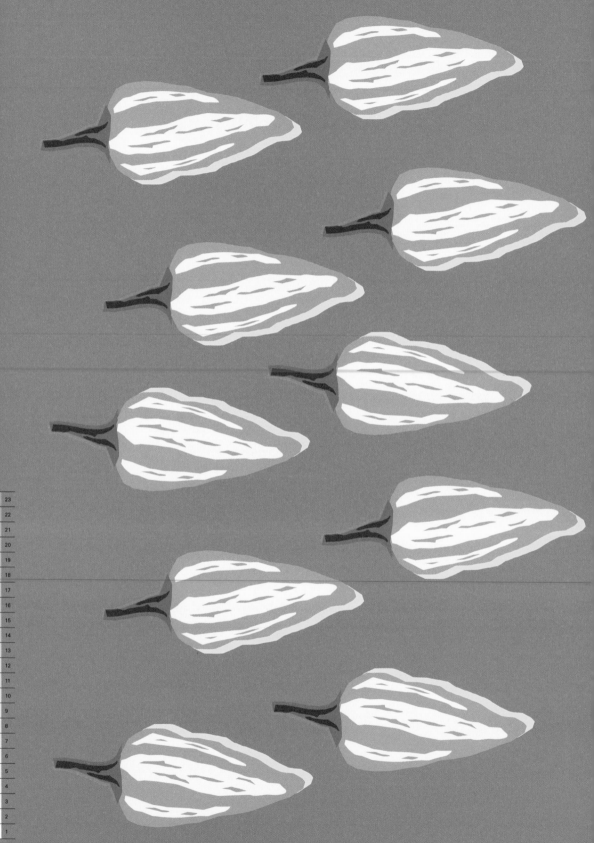

Fish Pepper

SCOVILLE HEAT UNITS 5,000 – 30,000

SIZE
4 x 1.5 cm (1½ x ½ in.)

ORIGIN
Caribbean

GROW
Easy to grow in containers, fish peppers grow up to 60 cm (2 ft) tall.

EAT
With a heat not unlike cayenne pepper, fish peppers have a subtle sweetness enhanced with lime juice or pineapple in a salsa, served with fish or shellfish.

FISH PEPPERS ARE striking for their initial pale cream colouring, via a recessive gene that causes albinism. Gradually they mature into a light green, with darker green striations. Although they are usually picked light green, if left to ripen fully, they turn orange with brown striations, then red. The leaves match the pods' stripiness by being variegated, with a mixture of green, grey and cream.

Fish peppers, which probably originated in the Caribbean, are African American heirlooms that predate the 1870s. They were used as a secret spice by late nineteenth-century African American cooks in seafood restaurants in Philadelphia and the Chesapeake Bay region, perking up the creamy white sauces served with lobster and fish (hence their name) without adding the telltale red specks of cayenne. The chilli's recent-ish resurgence is thanks again to the African American artist Horace Pippin, who gifted seeds to food writer William Woys Weaver's grandfather, along with those of the buena mulata (see pages 98–99). Although fish peppers are on the Slow Food Foundation's Ark of Taste list of endangered foods, they are increasingly available through seed-sharing exchanges.

Capsicum annuum

Hinkelhatz

SCOVILLE HEAT UNITS 5,000 – 30,000

SIZE
3 x 2 cm (1¼ x ¾ in.)

ORIGIN
Mexico/Pennsylvania, USA

GROW
The plant is bushy and
compact, growing up
to 60 cm (2 ft) max.
Cold tolerant.

EAT
Add to salsas, salads and
soups. Make pepper vinegar
for spritzing over sauerkraut.

THE NAME GIVEN to the round, tapered heirloom hinkelhatz pepper by its Pennsylvania Dutch growers – that is, German (*Deutsch*)-speaking immigrants, including Mennonite and Amish – who began cultivating it 150 years ago in the American state of Pennsylvania, translates as 'chicken heart'. Certainly the pods are shaped thus. The small, grape-sized peppers are covered in tiny wrinkles or bumps, and have a moderately to very punchy heat (the range in heat certainly makes this an interesting pod to try). Rarely eaten fresh, the hinkelhatz has traditionally been pickled; in Pennsylvania Dutch cooking it often flavours a pepper vinegar that is sprinkled over sauerkraut. The pods are usually red or yellow, though an orange variety is preserved among a small group of Mennonite farmers in Maxatawy, Pennsylvania. And such a rare chilli pepper it is, the hinkelhatz has been listed on the Slow Food Foundation's list of American regional varieties to be protected.

23
22
21
20
19
18
17
16
15
14
13
12
11
10
9
8
7
6
5
4
3
2
1
0

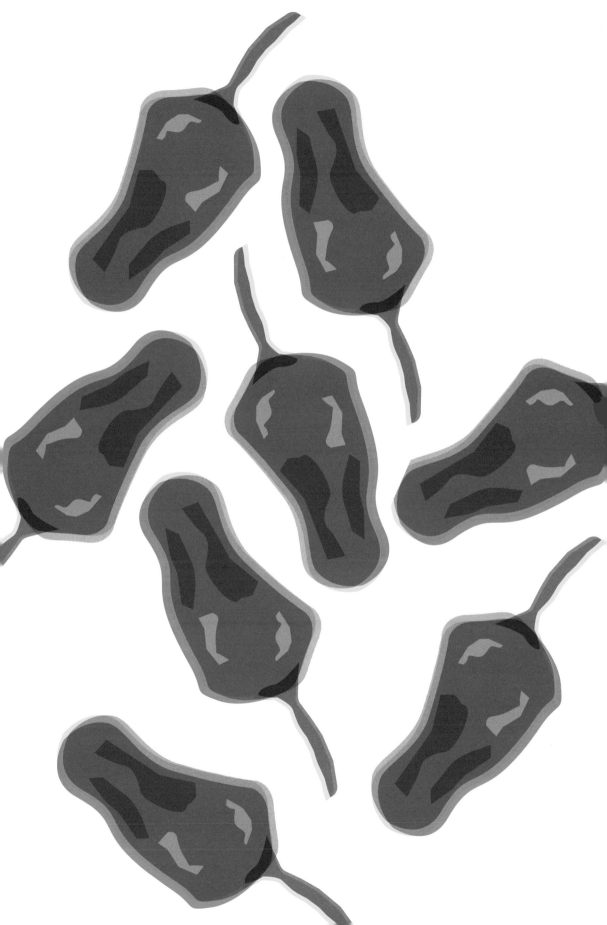

Capsicum baccatum

Christmas Bell

SCOVILLE HEAT UNITS 5,000 – 30,000

SIZE
7.5 x 5.5 cm (3 × 2 in.)

ORIGIN
Brazil

GROW
Sow in spring, planting
seedlings in a sunny and
sheltered spot. This is
a tall grower, heading
up to 1.5–2 m (4–6 ft),
requiring a good amount
of consistent full sun and
heat. Germination can
be slow.

EAT
Grill whole. Stuff. Dice and
add to salads and salsas.
Finely chop with garlic,
spring onion and a smaller,
hotter chilli and fold through
couscous with butter and
seasoning. Pickle the smaller
ones whole.

As ORNAMENTAL AS it is tasty (and potentially fiery), this is a
wonderfully unusual-looking wrinkled chilli pod: part flying saucer,
part Christmas tree bauble, with three or four flat wings.

Originally called Ubatuba Cambuci – its Brazilian name,
coming from two market towns where it is especially popular – the
Christmas Bell answers to many different names: ají flor, balloon,
bishop's crown, joker's hat and orchid among others. The peculiar
pods mature from a lime green to a brilliant orange or red.
The body of the pod has some significant heat with a little fruity
spice, but the wings of the fruit are sweet and mild. It is delicious –
if you can bear to eat such a beautiful thing.

23
22
21
20
19
18
17
16
15
14
13
12
11
10
9
8
7
6
5
4
3
2
1
0

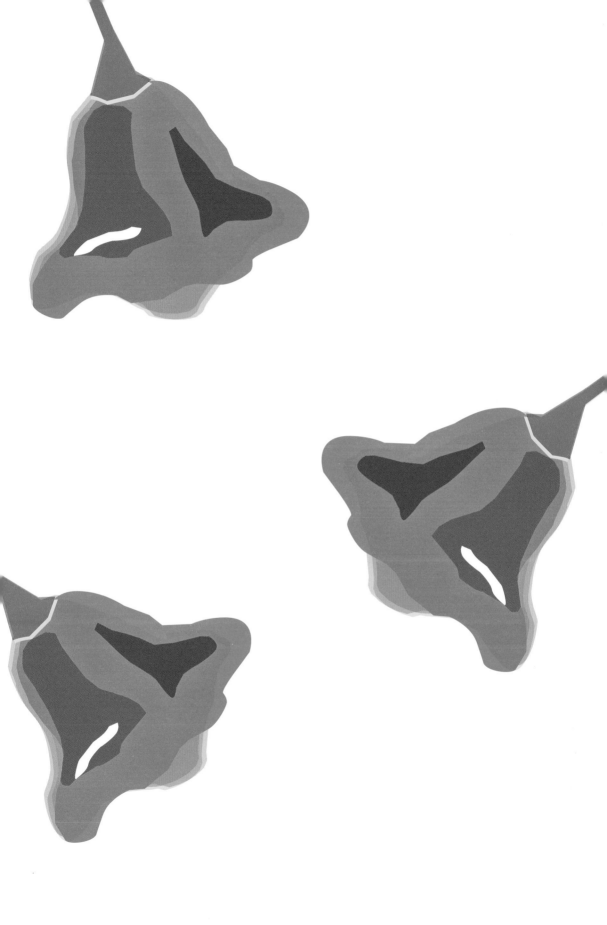

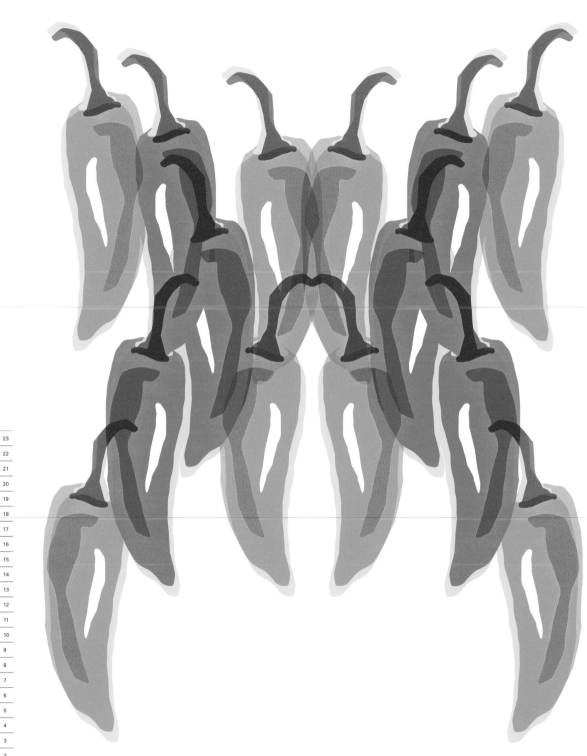

Capsicum annuum

Onza

SCOVILLE HEAT UNITS 5,000 – 30,000

SIZE
7.5 × 2 cm (3 × ¾ in.)

ORIGIN
Oaxaca, Mexico

GROW
Growing to a height of
75 cm (30 in.), the hairy-
stemmed onza plant is
an abundant producer in
full sun and well-drained
garden soil.

EAT
Use in the classic red
mole sauce. Use to make
chilli pepper jam. Pair with
cheese. Make a hot dressing
for squid.

WITH THIN WALLS, the onza pepper – slim and straight – is
particularly good for drying, though this is an all-round, all-purpose
chilli with a middling heat and a sweet taste. Originating in the
Sierra Norte region of Mexico's Oaxaca state, onza chillies start
green and mature a dark crimson red (the onza roja) or deep yellow
(the onza amarillo). This hot, musty pepper – resembling a small,
bright jalapeño – is used throughout Mexican cuisine, traditionally
in sauces, soups and salsas. An interesting and nutritious Oaxacan
sauce, *salsa de chapulines* – grasshopper salsa – is made by grinding
the toasted insects into a paste made of onza chillies, garlic and
tomates verdes (tomatillos).

Aci Sivri

SCOVILLE HEAT UNITS 5,000 – 30,000

SIZE
15 × 1.5 cm (6 × ½ in.)

ORIGIN
Turkey

GROW
A good grower in cooler, more northern climates, taking 90 days to mature.

EAT
Particularly good in Turkish and Indian cuisine. Add fresh to fiery chutneys, Turkish kebabs or fruity salads. Roast, purée, blend with salt, lemon and oil, and simmer to make biber salçası.

ACI SIVRI IS a centuries-old Turkish heirloom cayenne pepper with long, thin shiny crimson pods – almost with a paint-like gloss – that twirl and curl. The flavour is sweeter than standard cayennes with earthy and floral notes and a notorious but inconsistent pungency: some pods are mild, while others can have a ferocious heat. The productive plants can produce up to 50 fruits each and can be used fresh or dried.

Aci sivri peppers are traditionally used to make a rich red paste called biber salçası, which is a common element in Turkish cuisine, flavouring everything from dips, spreads and salads to stews, pilafs, marinades, *dolma* (stuffed vegetables), *börek* (filo pastries) and *pide* (Turkish pizza). When there is a glut of peppers in the autumn, it is not uncommon to see Turkish women preparing enormous batches of the paste for use throughout the following year.

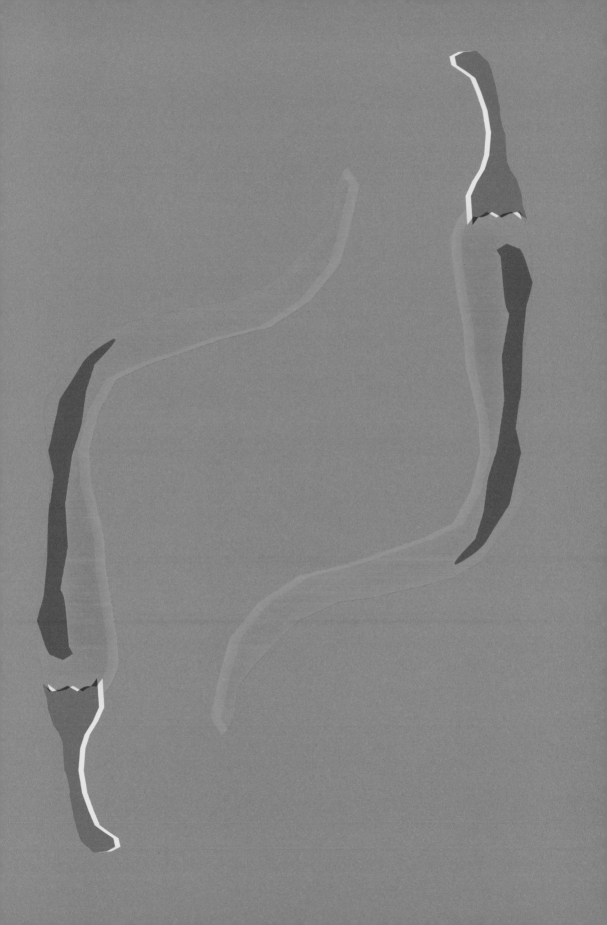

Manzano

SCOVILLE HEAT UNITS 15,000 – 30,000

SIZE
4 × 7 cm (1½ × 2¾ in.)

ORIGIN
Mexico/Peru

GROW
A slightly trickier chilli to grow, give support to this one, as it can grow up to 2 m (6 ft), and keep it out of direct sunlight. Though great for cooler climates, this plant is not frost resistant. It can live a few years and end up looking like a small chilli tree.

EAT
Make fruity salsas and chutneys, or stuffed peppers. Pickle, or roast and slice for *rajas* (roasted pepper strips). Turn into a spicy, fresh chilli sauce.

ALSO KNOWN AS ají rocoto, locoto, chile perón and chile caballo, the manzano chilli is a member of the *Capsicum pubescens* species: obvious from its furry stems and leaves, violet petals and black seeds. Originally from South and Central America where they grow at high altitudes, the little, round, apple-like pods (*manzana* is Spanish for 'apple') start green and turn a traffic-light range of red, orange and yellow. Indeed, the manzano almost looks like a sweet bell pepper, though the heat to any undiscerning pepper picker would immediately reveal it not to be the case.

The manzano's burn is longer, fuller and more all-encompassing than that of other chillies owing to higher levels of dihydrocapsaicin versus capsaicin (most chillies have it the other way round). Its crunchy, juicy flesh has a fresh taste – sometimes with a bean-like quality – and a well-balanced flavour-to-heat ratio.

The manzano is a highly desirable chilli to use both for heat and as a vegetable in its own right. The very thick flesh and skin is hard to dehydrate, so manzano chillies are mostly eaten fresh, chopped into salads or roasted and blended into salsa.

Chile de Árbol

SCOVILLE HEAT UNITS 15,000 – 30,000

SIZE
7 x 1 cm (2¾ x ⅓ in.)

ORIGIN
Mexico

GROW
This one requires full sun, growing up to 1.2 m (4 ft) in height, bearing heavy loads of slender, curved peppers all summer long.

EAT
Primarily used dried, and great in table sauces, soups, Thai curry, tacos, stir-fries and stews. Infuse olive oil with whole dried pods, or do the Mexican thing and add a couple of them to your next bottle of tequila. Make a pungent hot chocolate.

A SMALL CAYENNE-LIKE pepper that punches above its weight with its bright, clean heat, this Mexican chilli plant bears thin, elongated pods. The name means 'tree-like', an allusion to the branch-like hard stems. It is also known as 'rat's tail', a reference to the curly rattiness of the pods. As well as the solid heat, the chilli pod has a hint of nuttiness and smokiness, with a light grassy undertone. One cultivar ripens green to red, another red to purple. When dried, the pod retains its beautiful fiery colour.

This chilli is sometimes used in craftwork – wreaths, *ristras*, or decorative bowls – because the pods stay especially bright red after dehydration. Dried chile de árbol is also chef and food historian Maricel E. Presilla's chilli of choice for spicing hot chocolate because it delivers a clean heat without competing flavours. Salsa de chile de árbol is a fiery hot, deep red sauce made with lots of the dried, rehydrated peppers cooked with *tomates verdes* (tomatillos), garlic and salt and then puréed. *Torta ahogada* ('drowned sandwich'), popular in the Mexican city of Guadalajara, consists of a baguette-like roll filled with fried pork and then 'drowned' by being drenched with or plunged into a spicy, vinegary red sauce typically made with chile de árbol.

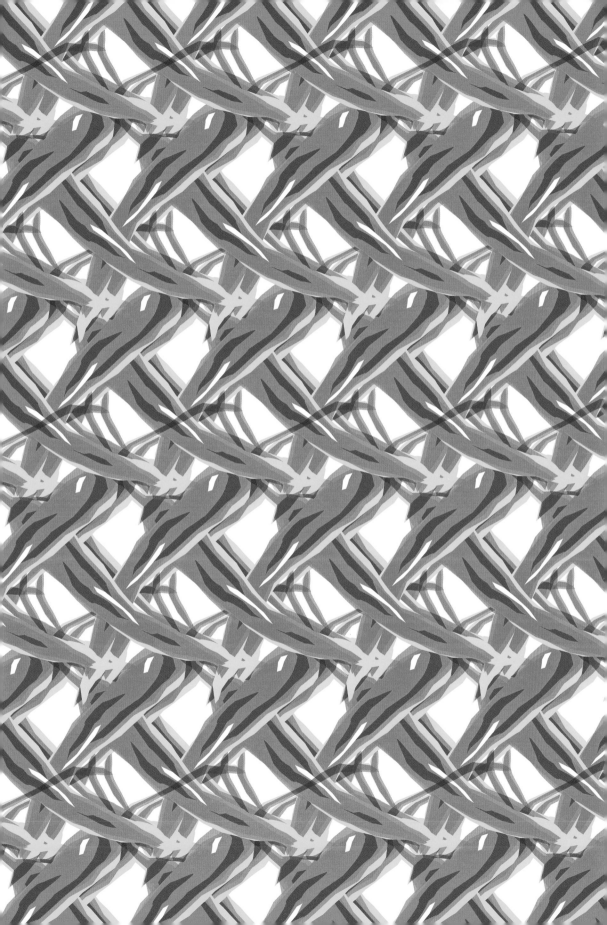

Capsicum annuum

Facing Heaven

SCOVILLE HEAT UNITS   15,000 – 30,000

SIZE
6 × 2 cm (2½ × ¾ in.)

ORIGIN
Sichuan, China

GROW
Sow early; this chilli
needs a good 30°C (85°F)
to germinate and can be
erratic. Grow in greenhouses
or polytunnels in colder
climates.

EAT
Use in stir-fries and curries.
Delicious in piquant pickles,
smoky chilli oil infusions and
sweet chilli sauces. Try in
Chinese food specialist
Fuchsia Dunlop's recipe
for Sichuan stir-fried potato
slivers with dried chillies and
Sichuan pepper.

A BULLET-SHAPED, medium-hot, fragrant chilli used in the cuisine
of China's Sichuan region, where it originates, the Facing Heaven
pepper's Chinese name, *chao tian jiao*, literally means 'skyward
pointing chilli pepper'. Its pods grow facing upward, rather than
down towards the ground, in tight clusters, making it an attractive
ornamental plant as well as a delicious culinary chilli.

These deep, rusty red chilli pods are remarkably hot and are
typically used dried. They are often tempered whole (fried in oil)
before being added to a dish, infusing the oil with the chilli's heat
and opening up its fruity, slightly smoky flavour, which is a hallmark
of Sichuan cooking.

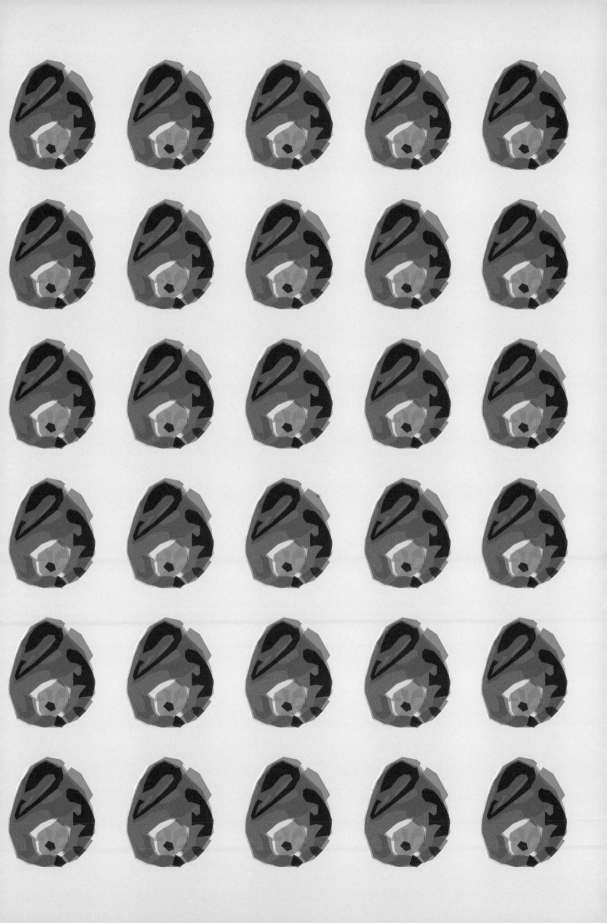

Capsicum annuum

Japones

SCOVILLE HEAT UNITS 15,000 – 30,000

SIZE
5 × 1.5 cm (2 × ½ in.)

ORIGIN
Japan

GROW
The ornamental plant is
attractive with white
flowers, growing up to
45 cm (18 in.) tall, with
pods appearing in clusters.

EAT
Use in stir-fries, peanut
sauces, Thai basil curry,
oil infusions and sauces.

A SLIM CAYENNE-LIKE pepper, the japones – also known as
santaka, or Japanese pepper – is a staple in Japanese, Chinese and
especially Szechuan and Hunan dishes. The name 'japones' may
refer to its Japanese popularity, or have come from the chilli term
capones, referring to a pepper that has been deseeded or 'castrated'.
Its moderate heat makes the pepper useful for liquid infusions such
as hot pepper oils and vodkas. Growing in heat as it matures, the red
form of the pepper is usually used, whole and dried.

The japones is a spicy chilli and brings a certain depth and
complexity to a dish. It is hot but not as hot as the ferocious, musty-
flavoured tien tsin chilli used in Chinese and Japanese cuisine, with
its maximum reach of 75,000 SHUs. Dried and ground, santaka
peppers are used as *ichimi togarashi* (ground red chilli powder) in the
Japanese 'seven-flavour' spice mix *shichimi togarashi* – whose other
components include sansho, roasted orange peel, black and white
sesame seeds, hemp or poppy seed, ground ginger and dried, flaked
seaweed (*nori*).

23
22
21
20
19
18
17
16
15
14
13
12
11
10
9
8
7
6
5
4
3
2
1
0

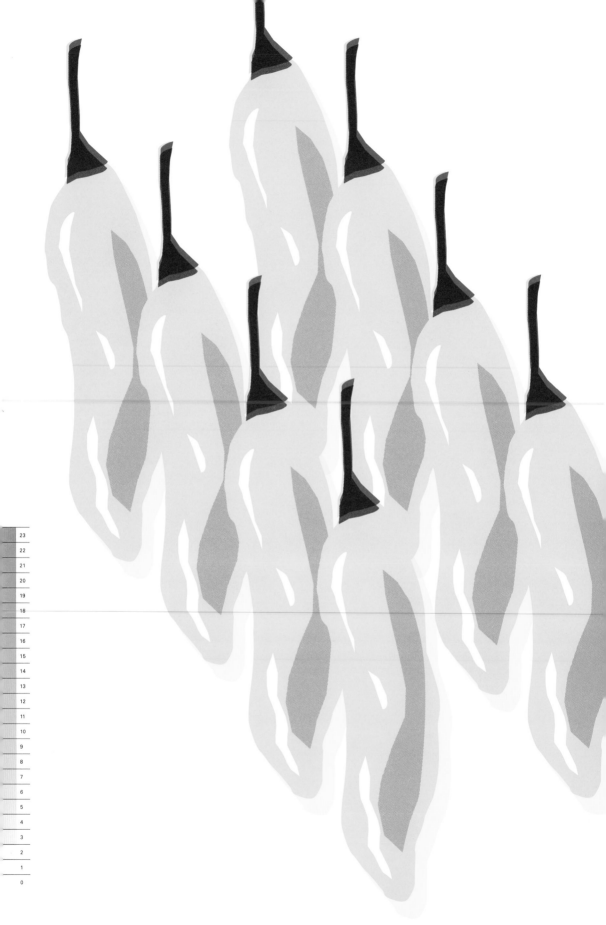

Capsicum baccatum

Lemon Drop

SIZE
7 × 2 cm (2¾ × ¾ in.)

ORIGIN
South America

GROW
Ideal for a pot on a patio or balcony or in a greenhouse (use a stake when it gets gangly).

EAT
Make a lemon, mango and shallot salsa, lemon drop jelly or marmalade, or Peruvian yellow pepper paste. Add to salads, salad dressings and stir-fried dishes. Chop into butter for fish. Also great dried.

HIGH-YIELDING LEMON DROP chilli pepper plants – from the aromatic *Capsicum baccatum* family with their notably wiry stems and green petals – grow upright to 2 m (nearly 7 ft) tall, with plenty of branches and relatively narrow dark green leaves. The shiny, wrinkled pods – which bear fewer seeds than normal – bulge and ripen from a pale green to a vivid bright yellow.

Also called the hot lemon and ají limon (not to be confused with the *Capsicum chinense* cultivar ají limo), the cone-shaped lemon drop pepper is a hot (though not overbearing), sweet, citrusy chilli with a fruity, fizzy, lemony flavour. It is used popularly in Peru as a dried and ground seasoning, and is rarely available fresh outside South America. If you're lucky enough to find a fresh one, or at least an imported jar of it in dried spice form, use it wherever a touch of lemon would wake up a dish.

Peter Pepper

SCOVILLE HEAT UNITS 25,000 – 35,000

SIZE
3 × 10 cm (1¼ × 4 in.)

ORIGIN
Louisiana and Texas, USA

GROW
An easy chilli to grow in
a garden or greenhouse
that gets plenty of sun.
The bushy plant grows to
1 m (3 ft) tall and 50 cm
(20 in.) wide, producing
a generous supply of peter
pepper pods.

EAT
Make a peter pepper salsa
or hot sauce.

NO GIGGLING AT THE BACK! This heirloom chilli is also known as the penis pepper and the chilli willy: when fully ripe, it seems to resemble the male member. (The pod is wrinkled, admittedly.)

The peter pepper is a surprisingly pungent one, first popularized by Texan journalist and chilli enthusiast Frank X. Tolbert, who wrote about 'little-known facts about little-known things that occur in little-known places'. It is often planted as an ornamental. The thick-walled fleshy pods are great fresh or frozen, or dried to make peter pepper chilli flakes.

American slang meaning of 'peter' aside, the chilli's name also recalls the English nursery rhyme in which Peter Piper famously 'picked a peck of pickled peppers', leading to the tongue-twisting conundrum: 'Where's the peck of pickled peppers that Peter Piper picked?' (A 'peck' is a unit of measure of dry volume equal to 16 dry pints and it is likely that the 'peppers' here are green peppercorns, not chillies.) The name Peter Piper is itself said to be inspired by one-armed Pierre Poivre, an eighteenth-century French horticulturalist who smuggled nutmeg plants and other spices out of the Moluccas.

Capsicum annuum

Japanese Hot Claw

SCOVILLE HEAT UNITS 25,000 – 40,000

SIZE
8 x 1 cm (3 x ⅓ in.)

ORIGIN
Japan

GROW
Grow this larger ornamental chilli that can reach up to 1 m (3 ft) tall in the ground or in large pots. Good for hot conservatory spaces or similar. The more pods you pick, the more pods will grow, so keep snipping.

EAT
Make *namasu* salad from daikon radish, carrots and chilli pickled in rice vinegar, salt and sugar.

THE DARK GREEN LEAVES and bright red, long, thin pods cluster in an upright manner, much like a claw. This Japanese chilli plant is known in its native country as takanotsume, and is an important ingredient in the spice mix *shichimi togarashi*. The thin-walled pods dry easily and are good for chilli flakes.

The Japanese Hot Claw is also known as the hawk's claw or poinsettia chilli, and with its clusters of lipstick-red, upright pods, the plant does have some resemblance to the famous poinsettia plant widely used in Christmas displays, and similarly makes a fantastic ornamental. The clawing nature of the impressive heat makes me prefer the more colloquial name I have used.

24
23
22
21
20
19
18
17
16
15
14
13
12
11
10
9
8
7
6
5
4
3
2
1
0

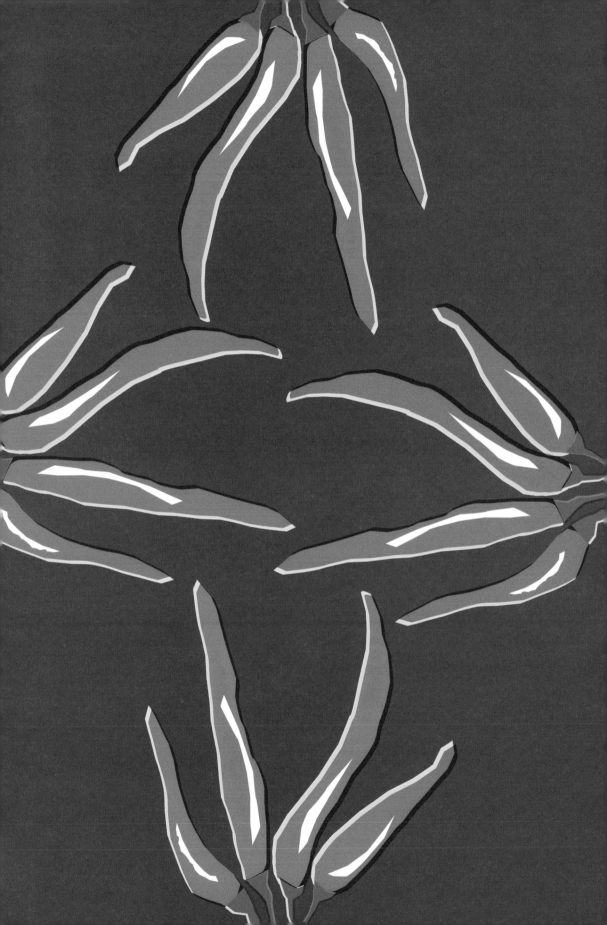

Joe's Long Cayenne

SCOVILLE HEAT UNITS 20,000 – 50,000

SIZE
30 × 1 cm (12 × ⅓ in.)

ORIGIN
Calabria, Italy

GROW
An easy to grow chilli plant, in warm soil, heading up to 1 m (3 ft). Not a windowsill pot, this one – it is best grown in the ground with support needed when it becomes gangly and top-heavy.

EAT
A great chilli for making sauces and jams. Perfect in a Thai curry. Make your own Joe's Long-infused vodka.

THIS CHILLI PLANT is not to be believed. Also known as Pinocchio's Nose, the long, thin nosey pepper pods grow to great lengths – up to 30 cm (12 in.) – turning from green to bright red as they mature. The flesh is thin, too, making this a great chilli pod to dry; it can often be seen in a *ristra* garland for this reason. The heat is well balanced and spicy, making this a good chilli with some heat for everyday eating and enjoying.

Cayenne peppers, whose name probably derives from a Brazilian Tupi word meaning chilli, are a group of long, thin, moderately fiery *Capsicum annuum* chillies. Cayennes became popular in the West from the seventeenth century onwards, mainly as the powdered spice cayenne pepper, used both to liven up European and American cuisine, and as a folk remedy for a range of medical ailments.

The Joe in the name of this cayenne seems to be Joe Sestito from Troy, New York State, who received the seeds from the Italian-Canadian seed-saving community in Toronto. The plant was originally bred in Calabria, Italy – the home country, of course, of Pinocchio.

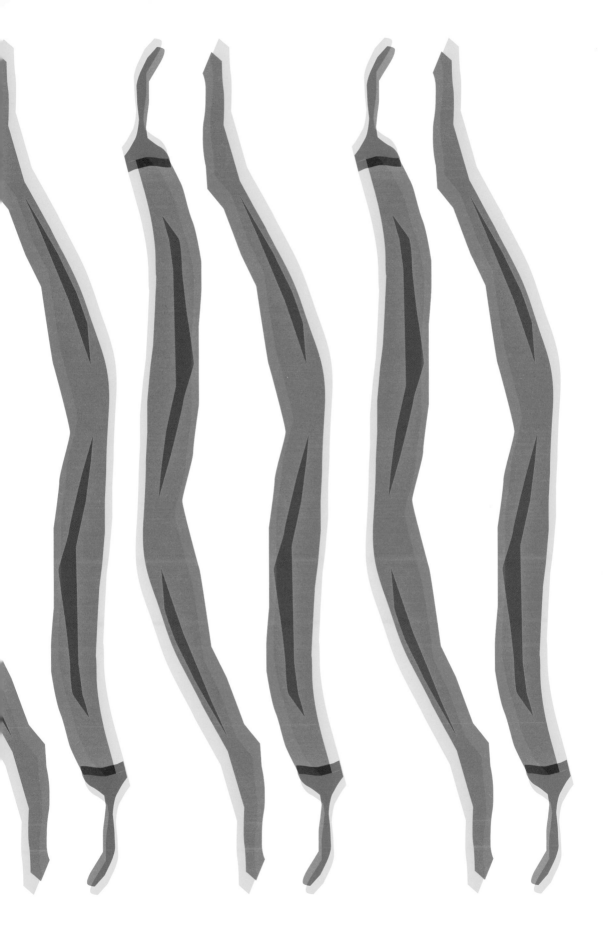

Capsicum annuum

NuMex Twilight

SCOVILLE HEAT UNITS 30,000 – 50,000

SIZE
2.5 × 1 cm (1 × ⅓ in.)

ORIGIN
New Mexico, USA

GROW
Easy to grow and hard to kill,
this edible ornamental can
be grown in small pots and
placed on windowsills or in
conservatories.

EAT
Finely chop and add to
potato salad. Mix with
garlic and chopped onion
and sprinkle over a tray
of vegetables for roasting.
Add to pasta dishes,
omelettes, curries and rice.

AN EYE-CATCHING BUSHY chilli plant with white flowers and
green leaves, the upright cone-shaped fruits start purple, then ripen
at varying rates to red, via yellow and orange, in a lively display that
looks like multi-coloured Christmas lights. The plant continually
provides fruit from summer to early winter – a relatively long time
for a chilli plant to be fruiting.

NuMex Twilight was initially developed by Paul Bosland
at New Mexico State University in 1992. It is one of the easiest
chillies to grow and therefore a great starter plant for a beginner.
The thin-fleshed fruits are small but pack a big, hot punch and can
be chopped into salads to add spice and colour; used in salsas, chilli
con carne and stews; or pickled whole.

Capsicum annuum

Rooster Spur

SCOVILLE HEAT UNITS 30,000 – 50,000

SIZE
4.5 × 2 cm (1¾ × ¾ in.)

ORIGIN
Mississippi, USA

GROW
A low-maintenance chilli plant, perfectly suited for small and large pots: easy to grow with plenty of sun and moderate watering.

EAT
Add to stir-fries. Dry and grind to make a homemade chilli powder. Make rooster spur sausage, if you can find a recipe.

AN HEIRLOOM VARIETY grown in Laurel, Mississippi, by seed-saver community member Virgil T. Ainsworth's family for more than a century, the rooster spur pepper bears pencil-thin, slender pods that mature to a fire-engine red, resembling a male rooster's spur and sticking up out of the low-growing, mounded foliage. The short, bushy plants are extremely productive and the fruit – though very small – is extremely hot.

The pepper enjoyed a brief moment of fame in 1978 when it was reported that a friend of President Jimmy Carter had thwarted Secret Service security checks to smuggle rooster pepper sausage into the White House. The Justice Department (where the friend worked) was then bombarded by formal public requests for a recipe for the sausage, a south Georgia local speciality made from pork, rooster spur peppers and secret spices – and rumoured to be an aphrodisiac. The recipe was never divulged, and the rooster spur pepper was almost impossible to find at the time, since it was grown only in people's gardens and not commercially.

It is alleged that President Carter asked for more.

Capsicum annuum

Pot Black

SCOVILLE HEAT UNITS   30,000 – 50,000

SIZE
4 × 1.5 cm (1½ × ½ in.)

ORIGIN
UK

GROW
Ideal for growing in pots in full sun on patios or windowsills. The plant will ultimately reach 50 cm (20 in.) tall.

EAT
An easy chilli to chop into stir-fries, curries, salsas, salads and even everyday sandwiches.

AN AUBERGINE-DARK SPECTACLE of a chilli, when fresh, the pot black is a new British-bred variety that ripens scarlet red. The plant is beautiful to look at and the pods are flavoursome with a clarity of heat and intensity. The bushy plant bears handsome purple flowers, gently blackened leaves and dramatic black fruit.

Capsicum annuum

Golden Cayenne

SCOVILLE HEAT UNITS 30,000 – 50,000

SIZE
12 × 2 cm (4¾ × ¾ in.)

ORIGIN
South America

GROW
A hot-weather crop, golden cayenne is easy to grow in well-drained soil and tolerant of humidity.

EAT
Dry the fruits and grind for an unusually golden chilli powder, or substitute for red peppers in your favourite chilli sauce recipe to make a hot golden-yellow sauce. Make a salsa verde with tomatillos, onion, garlic and coriander (cilantro) and pour over chicken enchiladas.

SMOOTH-SKINNED, BRIGHT golden fruits and creamy yellow flowers make this an appealing pepper for both the garden and the kitchen table. And with a Scoville heat level not to be sniffed at, and slightly hotter than most ordinary red cayennes, this is a great alternative cayenne to use, particularly in Creole and Cajun cuisine for added radiance of both flavour and colour.

With tapered ends and thick-walled bodies that twist, the pods are also a little larger than their ordinary red cayenne cousins, and they seem to get hotter as they grow bigger (as with all chilli plants, the heat can vary within the same plant). Golden cayennes are perfect to use in curries, salsas, jams, spicing up beans or in other traditional dishes from the Deep South. Interweave with red cayennes for a doubly colourful dried chilli *ristra*.

Capsicum annuum

Pusa Jwala

SCOVILLE HEAT UNITS 30,000 – 50,000

SIZE
10 × 1.5 cm (4 × ½ in.)

ORIGIN
India

GROW
With an umbrella-like plant habit, the plant grows to 50 cm (20 in.) in pots and will grow taller in the garden, though this pod is designed for commercial growing.

EAT
Add to masalas, chutneys, curries, kormas, vindaloos and tandoori dishes. Make a *tarka* (spiced fried onions for seasoning dal) by frying thinly sliced onions in ghee with garlic, cumin seeds, asafoetida and chopped fresh pusa jwala.

JWALA MEANS 'INTENSE FLAME' in Sanskrit, which is appropriate for describing both the heat and the tapering shape of these thin pods. Given that the pepper also resembles fingers, its alternative name – finger hot pepper – also rings true. Grown commercially in huge quantities in the Indian state of Andhra Pradesh, pusa jwala is one of the most popular Indian chillies, used regularly in both its lime-green immature state and ripened red. The wrinkled pods have a noticeably spicy heat with apple-ish undertones.

The arrival of chillies to India, via Portuguese traders in the sixteenth century, transformed the cuisine, appearing in masalas and chutneys, and encouraging the development of new dishes and cooking styles, including vindaloo sauce and tandoori-style meats. Indian chillies such as pusa jwala are now ubiquitous in the nation's dishes, as per the Indian saying (noted by food historian and chilli expert Dave DeWitt) 'The climate is hot, the dishes are hotter, and the condiments are the hottest.' Another saying hints at the benefits of eating sweat-inducing chillies in the hot Indian climate: 'Heat plus heat equals cool.'

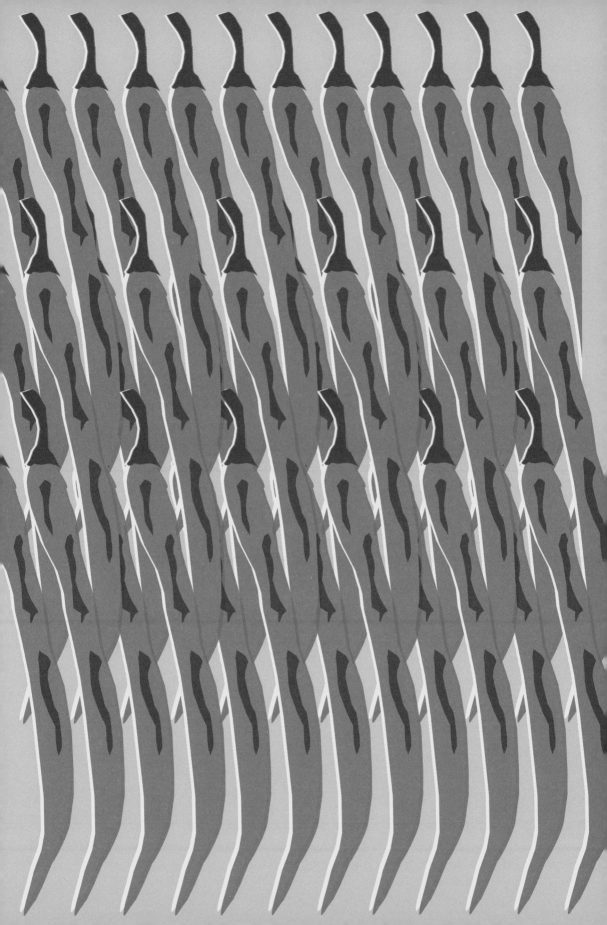

Capsicum baccatum

Ají Amarillo

SCOVILLE HEAT UNITS 30,000 – 50,000

SIZE
14 × 2.5 cm (5½ × 1 in.)

ORIGIN
Peru

GROW
Start these slow-growers early. Meaty, medium-sized pods grow from green to orange on tall, abundant plants. Try at different stages of ripeness for varying flavour (the slightly unripe pods have a fresh fruitiness).

EAT
Fry young peppers in olive oil with sea salt. Mix chopped ripe peppers with mayonnaise and serve with beans, fish, chicken or vegetables. Turn through salads. Roast, and add to eggs or quiche. Pickle.

THIS IS THE WAY to Amarillo: the pungent yellowy-orange chilli – sometimes ají escabeche or, colloquially, the yellow chilli or the yellow Peruvian chilli – has existed in Peru since Inca times, when it was introduced from the Caribbean by the Spanish.

Amarillo, of course, means 'yellow' in Spanish rather than referring to the Texan city of Neil Sedaka's song. The pods, which turn even yellower when cooked, are thick and meaty, with flesh that has flavour overtones of berry and snow pea and a bright, clean radish-like pungency and crunch. Its fresh, fruity, subtle heat distinguishes this chilli, allowing it to complement rather than overwhelm other flavours. Ají amarillo can be used in powder, purée or paste form. When dried the chilli is called a cusqueño, and has a flavour reminiscent of raisins.

The famous Peruvian restaurateur Gastón Acurio named ají amarillo as the most important ingredient in Peruvian cooking, where it is frequently found in salads, soups, sauces and ceviche. It is an essential ingredient in classic Peruvian potato dishes such as *causa rellena* (yellow potatoes layered with chicken) and *papa a la huancaína* (potatoes with a spicy cheese sauce).

Tabasco

SCOVILLE HEAT UNITS 30,000 – 50,000

SIZE
4 × 1 cm (1½ × ⅓ in.)

ORIGIN
Mexico

GROW
This popular chilli plant can be remarkably abundant in fruit if grown in a sunny position with good, moist soil. Go for the Greenleaf hybrid, which is resistant to the virus that almost completely wiped out the plants in the 1960s.

EAT
Chop fresh into salsas, salads and stir-fries; turn into homemade chilli jam, cooking oils and sauces. Pickle in vinegar. Use to spice up a Creole jambalaya.

THE TABASCO CHILLI – named after the Mexican state – is of course mostly known for what must be the world's most famous bottled hot chilli sauce, McIlhenny's TABASCO® red pepper sauce (the name is generally in caps), with its distinctive diamond label. American entrepreneur Edmund McIlhenny first packaged the sauce (in cologne bottles) in 1868 on Avery Island, Louisiana, where the wild pepper was originally imported from Mexico after the Civil War and where the sauce is still manufactured. To make the sauce, tabasco peppers are picked ripe, ground to a mash and then mixed with salt and matured in white oak barrels for up to three years, before being combined with vinegar and bottled. The sauce is now a global phenomenon, used in everything from French *steak tartare*, Irish oysters, Maltese *bigilla* broad bean dip and South African *frikkadel* meatballs, to the classic Bloody Mary with tomato juice and vodka.

Rarely sold fresh, though popular for home-growing, the small, conical, thin-fleshed tabasco pods grow pointing upwards, ripening from a greenish yellow to orange, then scarlet red. A single, sprawling plant can bear up to two hundred pods. On Avery Island, pickers gauge whether the peppers are ready by comparing them to a traditional tool called *le petit bâton rouge* – a small wooden dowel painted the correct shade of red. The fruity smelling pods – with a hint of pineapple – are noticeably juicy and have a lingering flavour, with a smidgen of celery, lettuce and spring onion.

Ají Charapita

SCOVILLE HEAT UNITS 30,000 – 50,000

SIZE
0.5 × 0.5 cm (¼ × ¼ in.)

ORIGIN
Peru

GROW
A bushy grower and an interesting variety given it is one of the first jungle chilli peppers to reach the world market, though it is still not easy to find outside its native region.

EAT
Use to make hot, fruity sauces, add to rice dishes, and chop over chicken and fish. Add a tropical twist to a fresh salsa.

THE TINY, SPHERICAL, thin-fleshed and very hot charapita pods – similar in size to the hotter chiltepín (see pages 164–65) – ripen from yellow-green to a rich yellow or red. Its name comes from the Peruvian term *charapa*, meaning jungle-dweller, as it is a wild variety found in the jungle close to the city of Iquitos, the isolated 'Capital of the Amazon'. It is also known as charapilla, tettinas de monk or Wild Peruvian. Chef, culinary historian and pepper aficionado Maricel E. Presilla describes the beautifully fragrant odour of the ají charapita as 'like ripe peaches and strawberries (some say apples), crushed herbs, and cut grass, with hints of wood and turpentine'.

Throughout Peru the chilli is tasted mostly in the form of a hot, sour sauce made with ají charapita and cocona fruit, the yellow-fleshed cousin of the tomato. The chilli's sharp, biting heat melds well with its citrusy, fruity, habanero flavours.

Capsicum annuum

Goat Horn

SIZE
15 × 1.5 cm (6 × ½ in.)

ORIGIN
Thailand

GROW
In cooler climates, grow in
a greenhouse as the pods
need time and warmth to
ripen, keeping soil moist.
Germination can take up to
6 weeks; otherwise, it is
an easy grower with a long
season.

EAT
Add to Thai curries and
Vietnamese pho. Pickle with
white vinegar, sugar and
slices of lime. Add to salads,
stir-fries and sauces.

THE DENSE GOAT HORN chilli plant grows up to 60 cm (2 ft)
and produces plenty of bright, glossy red pods. The long, winding
cayenne-like peppers – which really do look like goat horns – are
crunchy and juicy with a slight sweetness. This is a hot, flavourful
chilli, fruity and sweet, with a burning heat suitable for spicing up
Thai and other South East Asian dishes. As a cayenne-type chilli,
slender and tapering, it also dries and grinds well, making a fiery
hot pepper for use as a spice.

The Thai goat horn chilli is frequently confused with the
much milder, typically smoke-dried Chilean cacho de cabra
(literally 'goat horn'), which is similar in name but worlds apart
in shape and flavour, famous as the smoky, peppery element in
the Chilean spice blend called *merquén*, which can be added to
eggs, potatoes, soups and meats. Another 'goat horn', the Italian
corno di capra from Abruzzo, is a very mild, sweet pepper typically
served roasted or sautéed.

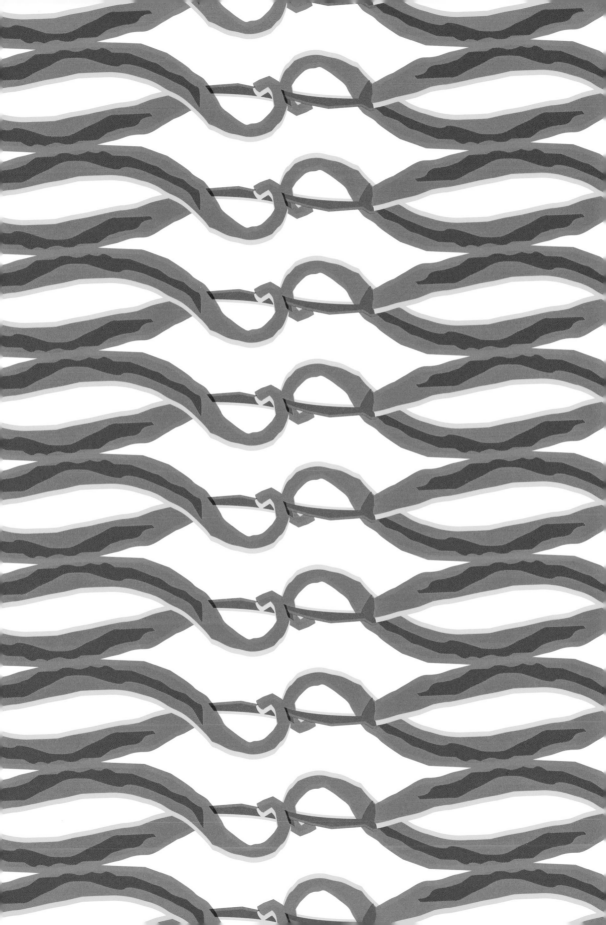

Capsicum annuum

Filius Blue

SCOVILLE HEAT UNITS 40,000 – 50,000

SIZE
1.5 × 1 cm (½ × ⅓ in.)

ORIGIN
South America

GROW
Once germinated, this
fairly low-maintenance
ornamental plant grows
quickly, maturing by about
80 days with beautiful bright
purple-blue chilli fruits.
A great show-off chilli pot
plant on patios.

EAT
Add to sauces, soups,
tacos, salsas, salads and
sandwiches. Make a
homemade Filius Blue
Sriracha-style sauce.
Freeze whole or dry.

LIKE DUKE ELLINGTON'S exotic and frolicking 'Blue Pepper
(Far East of the Blues)', the Filius Blue is a lively and jazzy little
number, a chilli bush plant bearing violet-blue, cherry-like pods
that pack a surprising punch. The pods are unusual among chillies
in that the riper they become, the more they actually lose their heat,
journeying as they do from a ferocious deep purple to a relatively
mild dark orangey flame red.

The small ornamental plant as a whole is rather beautiful:
the leaves are streaked with purple-blue and cream markings, the
flowers are white and purple, and the plant produces its dark purple
upward pods persistently and prolifically. Although this plant does
not grow very tall, it more than delivers in fruit and the clear heat
is highly desirable.

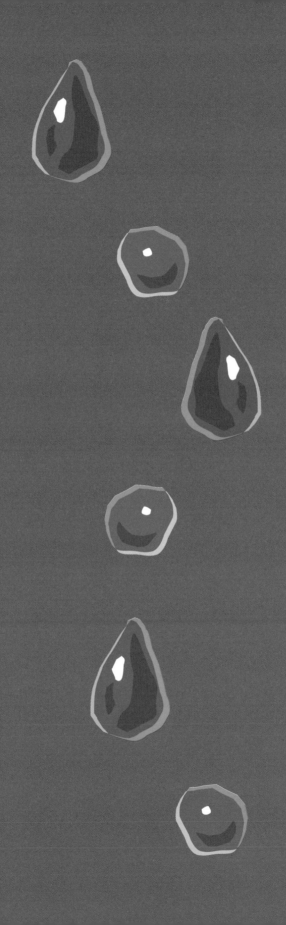

Capsicum annuum

Super Chile F1

SCOVILLE HEAT UNITS 40,000 – 50,000

SIZE
6 × 1.5 cm (2½ × ½ in.)

ORIGIN
USA

GROW
Short, bushy plants grow to around 30 cm (1 ft) tall. Suitable for hanging baskets, growbags and pots. Especially recommended for regions with short outdoor growing seasons.

EAT
A great pod for a classic American chilli con carne. Dry and use whole or ground.

SUPER CHILE F1 is the 'classic' chilli pod that most people imagine when they close their eyes and envisage a chilli: an elongated cayenne type that matures from light green to bright red – and with a clean, unfussy heat worthy of any hot dish. Super Chile F1 (also spelled Super Chilli) is an American hybrid, often grown as an ornamental because of its attractive, dense clusters of upright red and green pods and its reliable cropping, even in less-than-ideal conditions.

The wonderfully named Super Tramp, produced by Sea Spring Seeds in Dorset, England, is a de-hybridization (an open-pollinated – i.e. 'tramp' – variety that, unlike F1 hybrids, can be grown repeatedly from saved seeds) of Super Chile F1. The reliable earliness of both Super Chile F1 and Super Tramp makes them particularly good chilli plants for beginners to grow, especially in regions with shorter growing seasons.

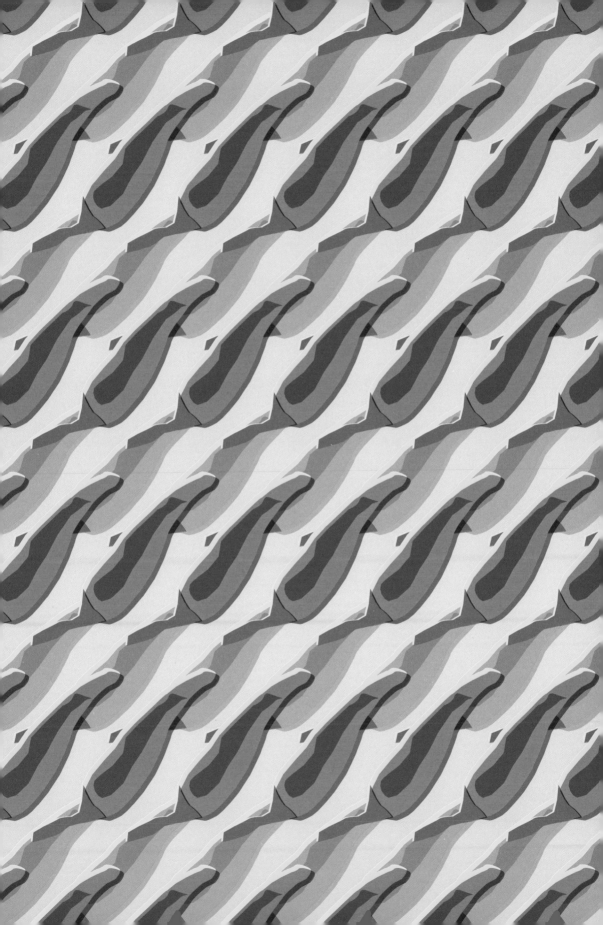

Pequin

SCOVILLE HEAT UNITS 40,000 – 60,000

SIZE
1.2 × 0.6 cm (½ × ¼ in.)

ORIGIN
Mexico

GROW
A prolific plant with small dark leaves that can grow up to 1.8 m (70 in.). Germination can be very difficult with this variety, and the plants are susceptible to disease, so not recommended for novice growers.

EAT
The pequin chilli is popular in salsas, hot sauces, vinegars and oils. Add a couple to a pot of soup for a kick. Dry and coarsely grind for flakes.

A LITTLE GOES a long way here with the sometimes-called mosquito chilli or rice pepper – a small, brilliantly red, intensely fiery pepper originating from northern Mexico. The name pequin itself means 'tiny' – which they are, not much bigger than a garden pea. Another nickname, bird chilli, derives from their popularity with winged creatures (birds are not affected by the heat-producing capsaicin). The pequin is often confused with the slightly smaller, hotter chiltepín (see pages 164–65).

Green pequins are usually sold fresh; ripened, red pequins are often dried. You can tell they are ripe because the pods fall off easily when they are even lightly brushed. Given they are so small, it is notable that pequin pods are full of seeds (some people still take them out). The pequin's flavour is pleasantly citrusy, with a touch of smokiness, and even nuttiness. The heat is strong but delayed (chilliheads call it a 'creeper'). This pepper is prevalent in South East Asian and Mexican cooking – perhaps most famously in Cholula brand Mexican hot sauce.

Capsicum annuum

Dundicut

SCOVILLE HEAT UNITS 30,000 – 65,000

SIZE
2.5 × 2 cm (1 × ¾ in.)

ORIGIN
Pakistan

GROW
Seeds for this commercially
cultivated chilli from
Pakistan are becoming more
widely available in the West
and should grow well in
optimal warm conditions.

EAT
Add dried to all kinds of
Pakistani, Indian and Thai
cuisine, and to marinades for
meat and shellfish. Use in
butternut squash soup, red
chicken or buttermilk curry,
or in spicy chutneys. Try in
the Pakistani delicacy *batair
masala* (quail curry).

POPULARLY USED DRIED and either flaked or in powder form,
the dundicut is the quintessential chilli of Pakistan – some say
the national chilli – developed in the Tharparkar region of Sindh
province. Of the impressive 180,000 kg of red chillies eaten in
Pakistan each year, the dundicut makes up over three-quarters
of the total.

Maturing from a fresh green to a deep ruby red, the dundicut
(occasionally spelled dandicut) pod is teardrop-shaped, with one
end pointier than the rounder other. The pods dry with a raisin-
like crimpling and a softer orange-red hue. This is a very hot chilli
– though not Scotch Bonnet level – with a deep, complex, fruity
flavour and a habanero-like aroma. Some have said there is even
a note of honeydew melon in the aftertaste.

Use it in all kinds of cooking if you are looking for a feisty,
fruity heat. One enjoyable surprise: I saw it in a recipe for gefilte fish
with lime and horseradish – gefilte fish being a normally very mild
traditional Ashkenazi Jewish dish made of ground white fish formed
into balls or patties.

28
27
26
25
24
23
22
21
20
19
18
17
16
15
14
13
12
11
10
9
8
7
6
5
4
3
2
1
0

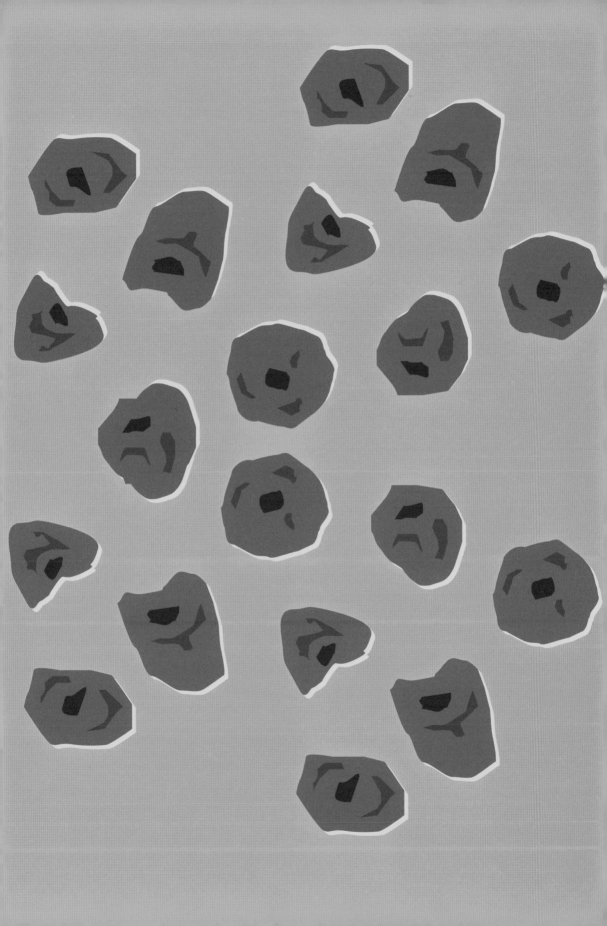

Capsicum annuum

Apache F1

SCOVILLE HEAT UNITS 70,000 – 80,000

SIZE
3 × 1.2 cm (1¼ × ½ in.)

ORIGIN
UK

GROW
Ideal for growing indoors
or in containers, heading
up to around 30 cm (1 ft).
Productive and fast growing.

EAT
Great for Thai or Vietnamese
salad dressings. Chop into
cooked kale with chunks
of blue cheese. Use dried
in linguine with crab meat,
lemon and garlic.

THIS PRODUCTIVE, MEDIUM HOT, neat and compact chilli plant grows attractive, bright scarlet bullet-shaped pods that are packed with seeds. A single one can produce well over 100 pods in the right growing conditions, before fruiting all summer long.

Early to mature and easy to grow, the Apache chilli has a devoted following among home gardeners, helped by its adaptability to all kinds of settings: greenhouses, patio containers, kitchen windowsills or straight in the ground outdoors. The plant has even picked up an RHS Award of Garden Merit along the way. This is a solid all-rounder of a chilli with impressive heat levels. The F1 in the name means the plant is an F1 hybrid – a cross of two pure lines to achieve a desired result. Creating F1 hybrids takes many years of preparation, often making the seeds more expensive.

Although it is named for one of the south-western Native American tribes, this chilli was actually developed by a British breeding company, Vegetalis.

29
28
27
26
25
24
23
22
21
20
19
18
17
16
15
14
13
12
11
10
9
8
7
6
5
4
3
2
1
0

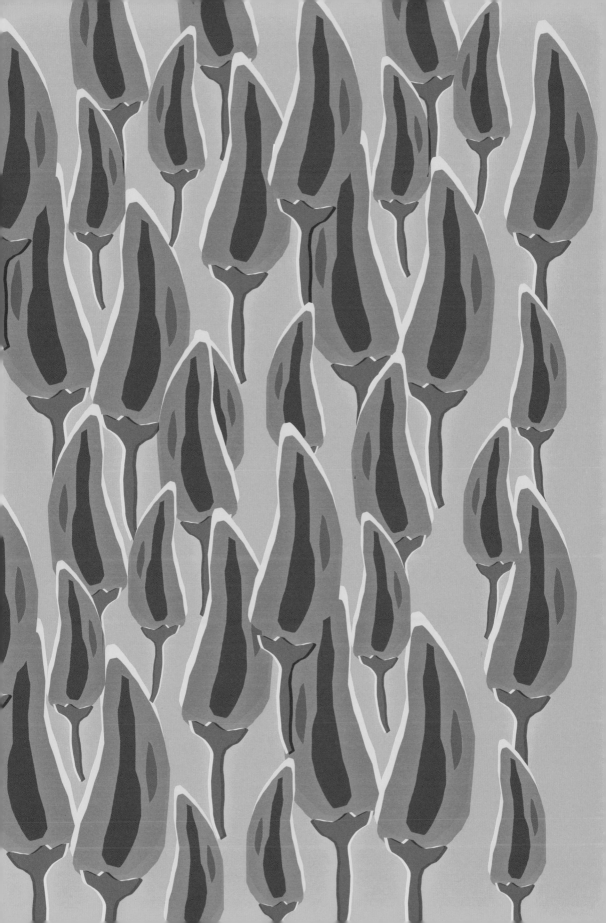

Capsicum annuum

Ring of Fire

SCOVILLE HEAT UNITS 70,000 – 85,000

SIZE
10 × 1 cm (4 × ⅓ in.)

ORIGIN
USA

GROW
An ideal pot grower on an outdoor patio or in a sunny conservatory, growing up to 45 cm (18 in.) tall with small green leaves. Great for novice chilli planters.

EAT
Great for a 'Ring of Fire' dip made with tomatoes, onions, tomato purée and black pepper.

SO FAR AS I KNOW, this chilli has nothing to do with the Johnny Cash song. Narrow, pointed and cayenne-like, it bears an impressive kick of heat, ten to fifteen times hotter than a jalapeño, hence the name.

Ring of fire pepper pods mature quickly and dry well thanks to their thin walls, which means this is a good pepper variety for making *ristras* and chilli flakes. The plant produces masses of the tapered chilli pods that start dark green and turn red as they mature. The pods can be picked and used at any stage of ripening. Compact, easy to grow and early to fruit, this is a great chilli plant for those short of both space and growing time, yielding a lot of fire for only a little effort.

29
28
27
26
25
24
23
22
21
20
19
18
17
16
15
14
13
12
11
10
9
8
7
6
5
4
3
2
1
0

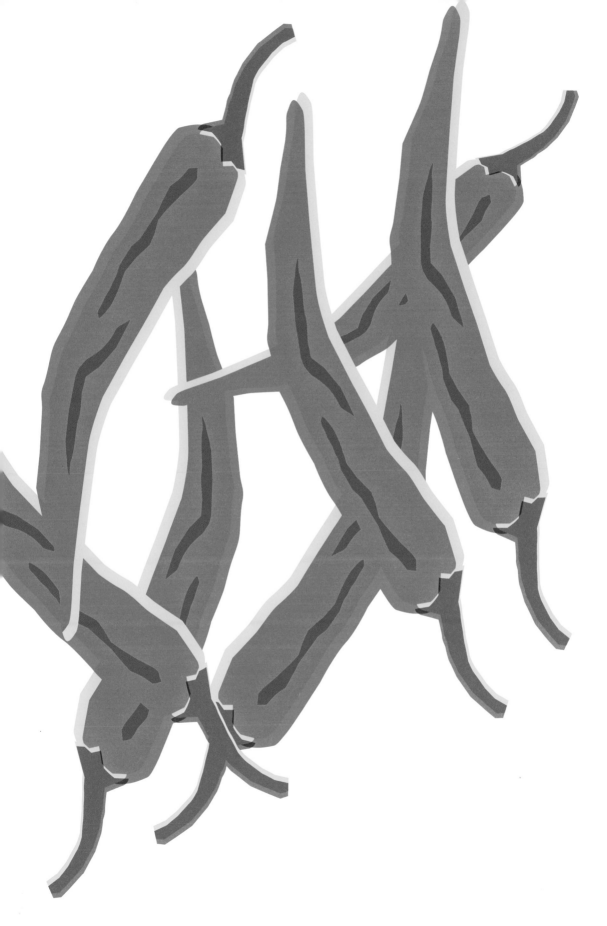

Capsicum chinense

Kpakpo Shito

SCOVILLE HEAT UNITS 35,000 – 90,000

SIZE
2.5 × 2.5 cm (1 × 1 in.)

ORIGIN
Ghana

GROW
These are medium tall, bushy plants that do well in the ground, or in larger pots. Support likely needed.

EAT
For a variation on shito sauce: crush a couple of handfuls of the fresh deseeded pods in a mortar or food processor (or in a Ghanaian *asanka* if you have one) along with a finely chopped onion and medium-sized root ginger and salt before shallow frying the resulting paste for 7 minutes. Serve with whole-grilled tilapia (or monkfish) and lime.

'SHITO' MEANS 'PEPPER' in Ga, as this chilli is a favourite grown in Ghana. With its sweet fragrance and spicy heat, this is a deceptively small habanero-type landrace chilli that packs an enormously hot punch for its size. This small zingy ball of a chilli pepper is regularly used in Ghanaian cuisine, including in fresh shito sauce – a varying mixture of tomato, onion and chilli pepper, often flavoured additionally with ginger, garlic, shrimp and anchovies.

The kpakpo shito sold in Ghanaian markets are usually picked when light green in colour, but can be ripened to red if desired. Seeds of the home-grown landrace variety are difficult to source outside of West Africa, except through seed-sharing exchanges. Sea Spring Seeds – the British breeder of the Dorset Naga – has developed three commercial varieties of the kpakpo shito: Pettie Belle, Raindrop and Cheeky. Pettie Belle is shaped like a tiny bell pepper, measuring about 25 mm (1 in.) in diameter with a heat level of around 38,000 SHU. The Raindrop is hotter at 88,000 SHU and shaped somewhere between a raindrop and a love heart, measuring only 20 mm (³/₄ in.) in diameter. The Cheeky, small and round and maturing to bright red at around 70,000 SHU, is so named because its deep lobes make it resemble a pert posterior.

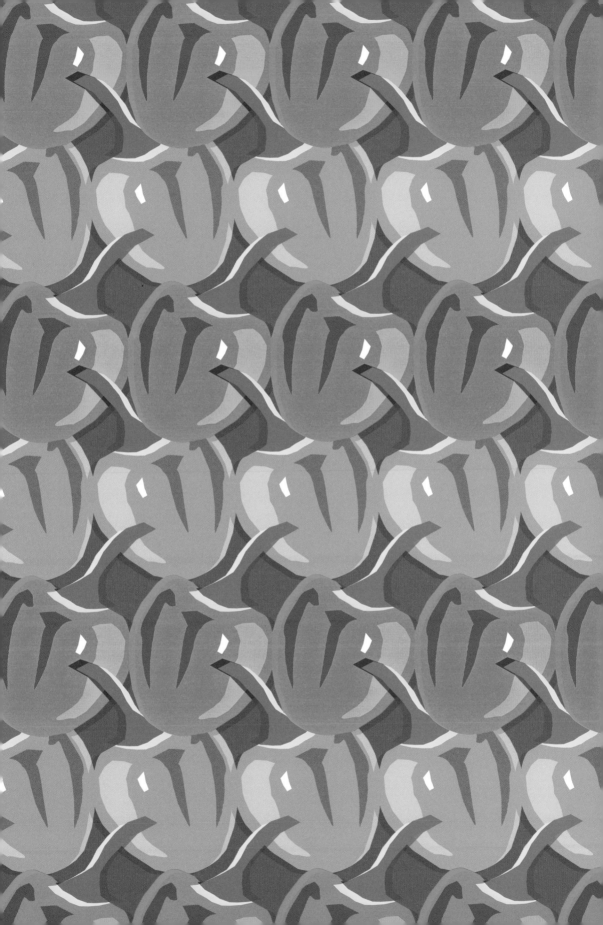

Chiltepín

SCOVILLE HEAT UNITS 50,000 – 100,000

SIZE
1 × 1 cm (⅓ × ⅓ in.)

ORIGIN
Sonora, Mexico

GROW
Plants grow to a height of
1 m (3 ft) and can live for
up to 50 years, though this
plant really flourishes in the
high Sonoran desert.

EAT
Add to soups, stews, salsas
and chorizo. Eaten sundried,
the pepper is often paired
with cheese or used in
sauces, or pickled with wild
oregano, sea salt and garlic.

THE JUNIPER BERRY-SIZED chiltepín pepper – also known as
tepin, tecpin or chiltepictl, among its many other names – is said
to be the oldest form of the *Capsicum annuum* species and therefore
the ancestor of many domesticated chillies. It was described in 1615
by Spanish naturalist Francisco Hernández, the first European to
collect American plants systematically. Its modern botanical name is
Capsicum annuum var. *glabriusculum* (meaning 'smoothish little object').
The pea-sized chiltepín pods are extremely pungent and very hot
with a distinctive smoky, dried-grass taste. The heat is numbing but
dissipates rapidly, helping other flavours in the food come through.
The chiltepín is most commonly available red or orange-red, but
yellow and brown wild varieties are also found.

The chiltepín (the 'tepin' part comes from the Aztec
Nahuatl word *tecpin* meaning 'flea' – tiny but noticeable) is used
extensively in Sonora, the region of northern Mexico thought to
be its birthplace. The chilli also has resonance in parts of Texas,
where – as the only wild chilli native to the USA – it has gained
the nickname 'mother of all peppers' and has been crowned the
'official native pepper of Texas'. Bottles of dried chiltepíns are
found in kitchens throughout the USA–Mexico borderlands, where
chiltepín has been used for centuries as both food and medicine.
Wild chiltepín harvesting is a seasonal ritual in many rural border
communities to this day (the harvesters, called *chilteperos*, head out in
late September). Despite efforts to encourage sustainable harvesting,
this historic chilli is in danger of extinction due to over-picking
in its natural habitat.

Malagueta

SCOVILLE HEAT UNITS 60,000 – 100,000

SIZE
5 × 1.5 cm (2 × ½ in.)

ORIGIN
Brazil

GROW
A good chilli for growing in pots, the plant should reach 50 cm (20 in.) high bearing many fruits, easily detachable when ripe.

EAT
Make your own malagueta pepper sauce: blend malagueta peppers together with raw garlic, onion, sugar and vinegar. Use to marinade a rack of lamb or chicken breast. Mix into Brazilian *farofa*, a ground manioc flour made from yucca root and served with smoked meat and spices.

THE BEST-KNOWN CULTIVAR of the least-known chilli species, *Capsicum frutescens*, is the tabasco chilli (see pages 144–45). Its close relative, the malagueta pepper – called pimenta malagueta in its native land, and piri-piri (from a general Swahili term for chillies, also used for *Capsicum annuum* African bird's eye varieties; see pages 174–75) in Mozambique and Portugal – is a Brazilian chilli plant with green flowers, upwards directed pedicles and small, hot, pointed fruits that ripen to vermilion red. The flavour is fruity and herbaceous. It is sometimes confused with the very similarly named West African cardamom-flavoured spice called melegueta pepper (a member of the ginger family, and also known as grains of paradise).

Popular throughout Brazil, Portugal, the Caribbean and Mozambique, in Brazil the pepper is a special favourite of the Bahia state where it is used in the Afro-Brazilian cuisine. Malagueta chilli oil and chilli sauces can be found in bars and restaurants throughout the country as a condiment, and the chilli is the go-to for spicing up Brazilian soups and stews.

30
29
28
27
26
25
24
23
22
21
20
19
18
17
16
15
14
13
12
11
10
9
8
7
6
5
4
3
2
1
0

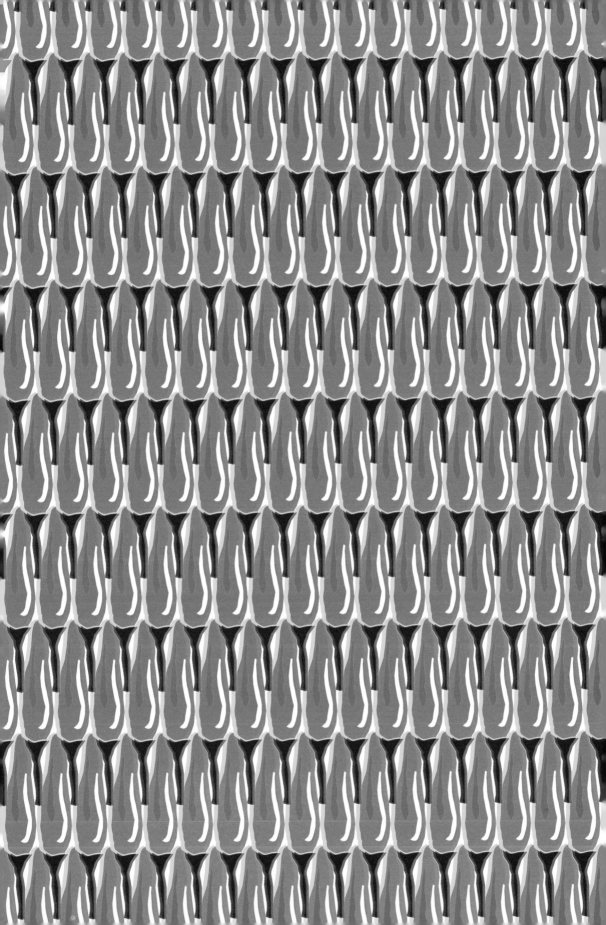

Capsicum annuum

Prairie Fire

SCOVILLE HEAT UNITS 70,000 – 100,000

SIZE
3 × 1 cm (1¼ × ⅓ in.)

ORIGIN
Mexico

GROW
Ideal for first-time growers looking for a hot plant. Grow in pots on windowsills or balconies, or use in landscaping a garden. The plant grows quickly up to 15 cm tall (6 in.) and will not need supporting.

EAT
Great for making a sweet chilli jam or snipping into salads for a punch of heat. Use fresh or dried in stir-fries, curries or salsas. Good for freezing whole.

THIS BUSHY AND PROLIFIC dwarf plant grows masses of tiny, colourful upward-pointing pods above the foliage, ripening from chartreuse and cream through to yellow, orange and red. A single prairie fire plant can bear pods with all these colours at once, making the overall effect extremely eye-catching – it is sometimes called Christmas Pepper because the pods resemble Christmas lights – and won the prairie fire an RHS Award of Garden Merit in the UK. For an ornamental, the blazing wildfire heat level is surprising, as is its accompanying fruity tang and spicy notes (hot ornamentals tend to be just heat without subtlety of flavour).

Use prairie fire chillies to garnish an extra-fiery Prairie Fire shot of hard liquor laced with hot sauce. Historically drunk in bar-rooms of the American Midwest as a forfeit for lost bets, the Prairie Fire can be made with whiskey, tequila, rum or even sake, flavoured with a generous amount of hot sauce.

Siling Labuyo

SCOVILLE HEAT UNITS 80,000 – 100,000

SIZE
2.5 × 0.7 cm (1 × ⅓ in.)

ORIGIN
The Philippines

GROW
Preferring warmer climates,
this plant, which can reach
1 m (3 ft), can be grown in
polytunnels or greenhouses
in cooler temperatures.

EAT
Turn into dips, ketchups
or sauces; add to soups,
stews and curries. Cook in
a Bicolano *kinunot* rice dish
with crab or stingray. Pickle.

LIKE THE TABASCO and malagueta chillies, the siling labuyo
is one of a small number belonging to the species *Capsicum frutescens*,
whose cultivars tend to be compact growers with ovate leaves,
making good container plants.

Literally meaning 'wild chilli' in Tagalog – one of the
many languages of the Philippines – this small red chilli (there
are also yellow and purple varieties) is a scorcher. The intensely
piquant, thin-skinned pod has an oval shape that tapers towards
its rounded tip. It features especially in the spicy cuisine of the
Bicol and Mindanao regions in the central Philippines. One of
the most common uses of this chilli is in a spicy condiment made
with vinegar, ginger, onion and garlic. The leaves of the plant can
be used in seafood soups and the hearty chicken *tinola*, a Filipino
soup made with papaya, ginger and lemon. It is also used as a
traditional medicinal plant in the Philippines. A recent influx of
commercially imported peppers such as African bird's eye chillies
(see pages 174–75), falsely sold as siling labuyo, threaten the survival
of this chilli in its native home. For this reason, siling labuyo is
on the Slow Food Foundation's Ark of Taste list of endangered
traditional foods.

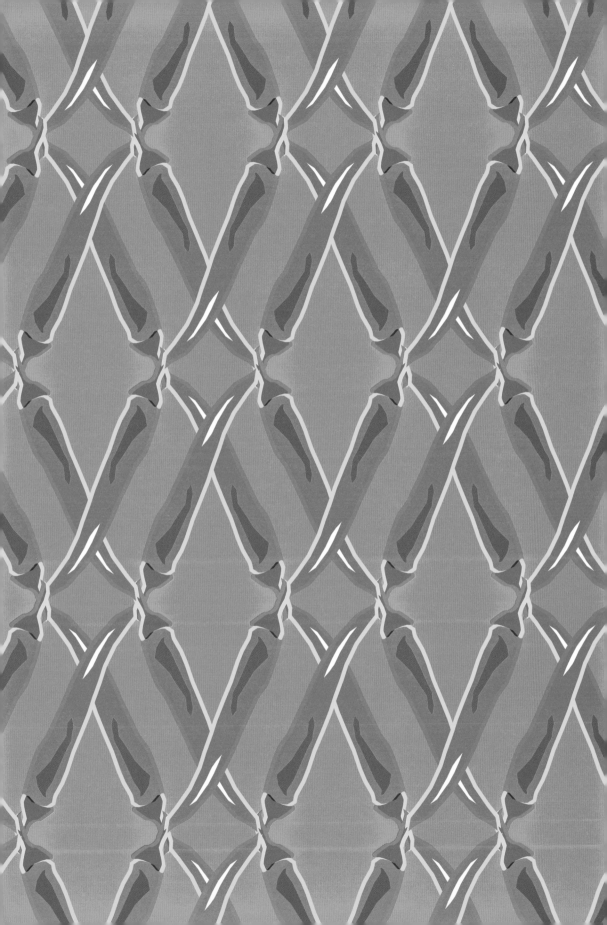

Turtle Claw

SCOVILLE HEAT UNITS 90,000 – 100,000

SIZE
4 × 1 cm (1½ × ⅓ in.)

ORIGIN
Bolivia

GROW
A difficult seed to germinate,
the beautiful, prolific plant
grows up to 60 cm (2 ft) with
umbrella-shaped foliage.

EAT
A really versatile chilli pod
for lifting up sauces, salsas,
soups and stews.

THE SMALL, BUMPY, elongated fruits of the Bolivian turtle claw perhaps look more like caterpillars than turtle claws, though the heat has a classic habanero-type hit and 'clawing' certainly describes the feel at the back of the throat. Varying in colour from white cream to yellowy green, the instantly hot pods have a crisp, sweet taste with a well-balanced lemony uplift.

In Bolivia a similar but much hotter chilli is the cream-coloured aribibi gusano ('gusano' means 'worm' in Spanish), known locally as the caterpillar pepper. In Britain, Submarine is another hotter variety (135,000 SHU) developed by Sea Spring Seeds from the turtle claw, selected for higher yields, shiny bright yellow pods and an outstanding perfume.

Joy Michaud of Sea Spring Seeds shares a great tip for testing the heat of chillies in general, and chillies at this point on the Scoville scale are where I like to start using it. Moving the pod away from you (to avoid any spitting if it is juicy), break the chilli in two at the middle. Press your little finger into the broken edge of the chilli wall, then press the same finger onto your tongue. The result will be a localized sensation of (hopefully) bearable heat, avoiding the distress of biting into a chilli pod that is too hot for you.

African Bird's Eye

SCOVILLE HEAT UNITS 100,000 – 225,000

SIZE
3 × 0.7 cm (1¼ × ⅓ in.)

ORIGIN
Africa

GROW
The bushy plants grow fruit prolifically, if a little slowly, so start seeds as early as possible in spring. Plants grow to 1 m (3 ft) in the ground but also work well in more constrained spaces.

EAT
Add to soups, stews, salsas and sauces. Pair with pear in a hot, fruity chilli chutney. Make small slits in the chillies and use in Gujarati hot, sweet and sour mango soup.

THE BIRD'S EYE is a classic case of chilli anarchy. Like cayennes and habaneros, the bird's eye is a type of chilli rather than a single variety – and there is a lot of confusion out there, with various regional names often applied interchangeably to similar-looking chillies from different species. An African bird's eye chilli (the *Capsicum annuum* bird's eye we have chosen to celebrate here) could elsewhere be called, accurately or not, a boonie pepper, a lombok rawit, a Thai Dragon, a kochchi, a kanthari mulagu…

The African bird's eye is also known as piri-piri, from a redoubling of the Swahili word for pepper, lending its name to the famous tangy, spicy Portuguese-influenced chilli sauce (also called peri-peri) made from the peppers in southern Africa, especially in Mozambique and Angola. The upward-pointing pods are small, thin-skinned and blunt-ended, in common with all bird's eye types, and mature to red, sometimes purple. Their flavour is not something special to write home about, but the heat is certainly memorable.

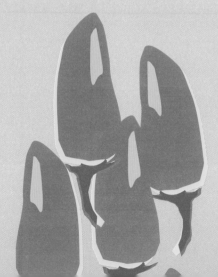

Capsicum annuum

Prik Kee Nu

SCOVILLE HEAT UNITS 100,000 – 250,000

SIZE
4 × 0.7 cm (1½ × ⅓ in.)

ORIGIN
Thailand

GROW
This prolific producer grows well in a pot to about 60 cm (2 ft) tall. Suited to a consistently humid and warm environment.

EAT
Make *prik nam pla* (Thai dipping sauce): mix 8 sliced prik kee nu pods, 6 tbsp Thai fish sauce, 5 tbsp fresh lime juice, 2 large garlic cloves and 1 thinly sliced shallot.

WITH A NAME literally meaning 'mouse-dropping chilli' in Thai, the prik kee nu pod is – as its name suggests – tiny. Popular in Thailand and other South East Asian countries including Indonesia, Malaysia, Singapore and the Philippines, prik kee nu is also prevalent in Keralan cuisine. Western chefs sometimes call prik kee nu peppers 'scuds', supposedly a reference to the infamous Soviet Scud ballistic missiles and the explosive, unexpected blast of heat these tiny red chillies can deliver. Michelin-starred British chef David Thompson's recipe for *geng som pla* (a thin, sour Thai fish curry), for example, includes 'scuds (optional): a few'.

Starting green, the pods mature to a bright red with an orange hue in the middle of the growth. The pods grow in clusters that droop down. Eaten green, they are very strong and have an immediate bite to them; the red pods have a delayed ignition. Though the flavour is not too much to comment on, the heat is glowing and long lasting, particularly the prik kee nu suan variety, providing a great lift of heat for Thai dishes such as *tom yum goong* (hot and sour shrimp soup), *som tam* (green papaya salad) and *gai pad gaprow* (chicken stir-fry with holy basil).

Bahamian Goat

SCOVILLE HEAT UNITS 100,000 – 300,000

SIZE
4 × 5 cm (1½ × 2 in.)

ORIGIN
Bahamas

GROW
The Bahamian Goat can take a while to germinate. The robust plant grows up to 1 m (3 ft) tall and can be a prolific pod producer.

EAT
A great, extremely hot chilli to cook with: turn into a sauce or salsa or use in Jamaican jerk cooking, barbecues or rubs. A little can be used fresh in salads. Or make a traditional Bahamian chicken *souse* (soup).

SIMILAR IN SHAPE to the related Scotch Bonnet (see pages 190–91) and other habaneros, the Bahamian Goat (unsurprisingly) originates from the Bahamas. The presence of 'goat' in the name has multiple explanations: it could be the goat-like kick of the heat or the faint whiff of goat when the chilli is cut open; the fact that the chillies are typically grown where goats forage in the Bahamas is sometimes also mentioned.

These strangely beautiful pods mature to a pale peach colour, some producing a scorpion-like tail at the base. The chilli has an upfront, fresh, fruity flavour with hints of apricot and tropical fruit, and a powerful, sweat-inducing heat that builds on the tongue.

In Haitian Vodou and related Caribbean folk religions, the death *loa* (spirit) Maman Brigitte is said to drink rum infused with 21 goat peppers. Worshippers drink this fiery concoction during ceremonies to prove their devotion, and as a sign of possession by Maman Brigitte, since an ordinary person would not be able to tolerate the heat.

Datil

———

SCOVILLE HEAT UNITS 100,000 – 300,000

SIZE
8 × 2.5 cm (3 × 1 in.)

ORIGIN
Florida, USA

GROW
This plant grows well in warm conditions (which is why they are so prolific in Florida). In cooler climates, they can grow in a greenhouse.

EAT
Chop and throw into all kinds of dishes and salads. Bottle as a vinegar. Make St Augustine's signature Minorcan clam chowder using tomatoes, vegetables, clams and seafood stock.

ALSO KNOWN AS yellow lantern chillies, datils – the word means 'date' in Spanish – are uncannily shaped liked date fruits, beginning small and green and growing into deep yellow and orange pods. The initial sweetness of the chilli makes way for a fresh, citrusy flavour. The heat is akin to a habanero, but the sting is highly pleasurable.

Datil peppers are the favourite chilli of St Augustine, Florida, where they have been widely adopted by the city's Minorcan population. Descendants of indentured servants from the Spanish Balearic Islands, the Minorcans have made datil pepper central to Old Florida cuisine since the 1800s with recipes such as datil pepper vinegar, relish, jellies, mustards and a famous tangy and spicy datil pepper sauce ('bottled hell'). Datil peppers are often eaten with north-eastern Floridian dishes such as fried shrimp, mullet, Minorcan clam chowder, cornbread and okra – and even datil fudge.

It is unclear whether this bright fruity chilli originated in Minorca and was brought over by early immigrants, or was bred locally in Florida; another theory is that the plant was brought over in 1880 by a jelly maker from Chile called S. B. Valls. Since most datil peppers are grown in Florida, they are susceptible to the hurricanes and floods in the region, and for this reason the Slow Food Foundation has listed the datil as an endangered American heritage food.

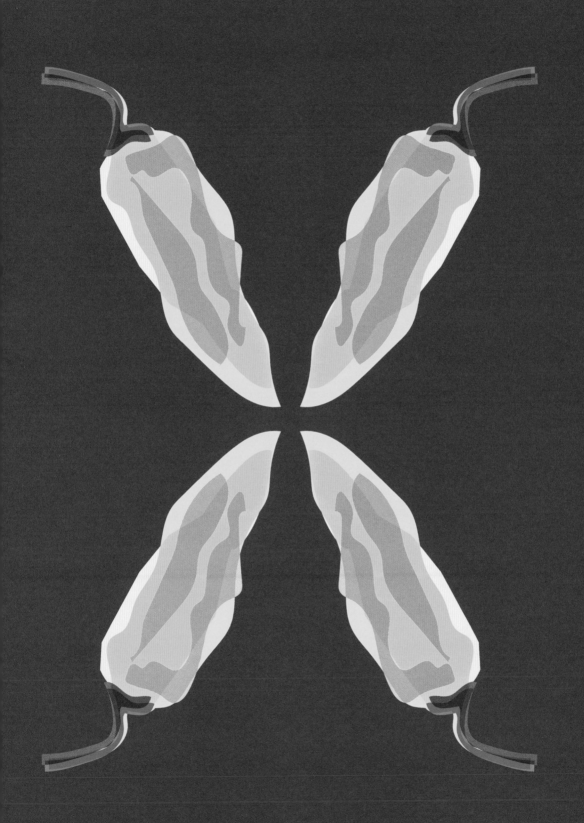

Fatalii

SCOVILLE HEAT UNITS 100,000 – 300,000

SIZE
8 × 5 cm (3 × 2 in.)

ORIGIN
Central African Republic

GROW
A relatively easy and hot
chilli to grow, the plant
can grow up to a metre,
requiring plenty of sun
(or a greenhouse in cooler
climates). This chilli has
a high germination rate.
Pick early.

EAT
Makes a great, flavourful
and hot salsa. Chop the
pepper (thinly!) into
sandwiches. Dry the thin-
walled chilli pods and grind
for a powerful chilli powder.
Add to yellow or fruit-based
sauces for a hot, fruity kick.
Pickle.

KNOWN FOR ITS strong heat and citrus flavour alike, the fatalii
(we are sticking with the yellow variety here) is one of the few
African *Capsicum chinense* pods. The thankfully-not-fatal fatalii chilli
nevertheless has a throat-hitting, tongue-burning habanero-like
heat with a delayed, lingering, stinging burn that is likely to induce
sweat and tears: it is a 'creeper' in chillihead parlance, with a few
claims for higher Scoville ratings of 400,000 and even 500,000 SHU.
The fatalii's heat characteristics hits different parts of the mouth
at different times; different people will respond in different ways,
though it is generally agreed the sweet fruitiness – coming up trumps
in heat and flavour alike – are this chilli's chief charms.

It is worth stressing that this is certainly not a chilli for the
fainthearted, but likewise not one to be missed if you are climbing
your way up the Scoville scale. There are other kinds of fatalii worth
trying: chocolate, red, white and peach.

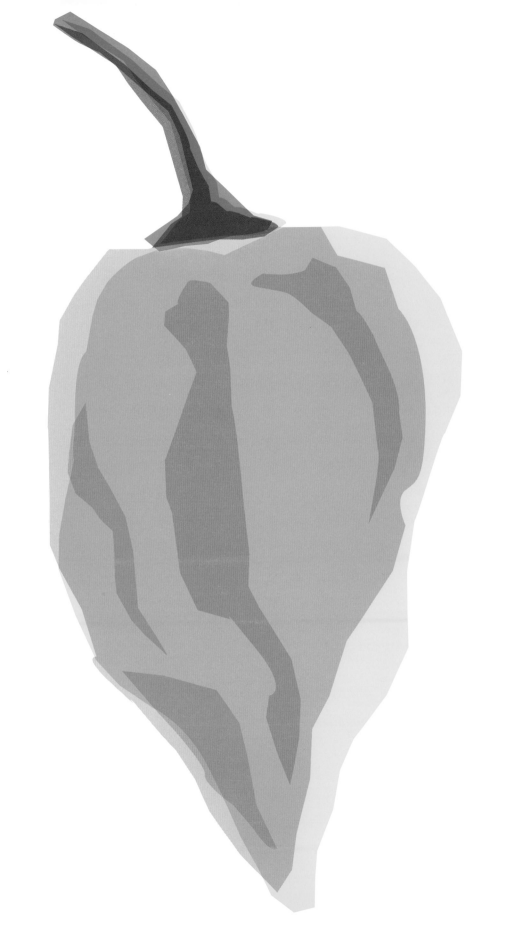

Capsicum chinense

Peruvian White Lightning

SCOVILLE HEAT UNITS 150,000 – 300,000

SIZE
5 × 2 cm (2 × ¾ in.)

ORIGIN
Peru

GROW
Small bushy plants that
head up to 45 cm (18 in.)
tall yield plenty of creamy
white lantern pods.
A difficult one to grow,
this habanero needs optimal
and consistent growing
conditions.

EAT
Use fresh white lightning
in salsas, salads or a sweet
lychee chilli dip. Use dried
in creamy white hot sauces.
Go rogue: chop a little into
vanilla ice cream for a wild
flavour contrast.

STARTING LIME GREEN, the ornamental ovoid pods of this
rare and beautiful habanero type ripen pearly white – standing
out from the rest of the red chilli crowd. The crunchy pods have
a smoky, sweet, citrusy taste – a flavour as unexpected as the colour
palette – and the potent heat is on for such an innocuous-looking
chilli (it almost reaches the level of the one-time world's hottest,
Red Savina, see pages 196–97, and some say it can go even higher).
The bean-like pods are possibly a little harder to bite than most
chillies, and due to their tiny size a good number can fit comfortably
in a handful (helpful during harvesting given the plant is so
productive).

Were you to encounter this chilli disguised in a white sauce,
like an infinitely more ferocious version of white fish pepper
(see pages 106–07), it might indeed feel like you had been struck
by lightning, should you taste it unawares. Which makes this a
good moment for a reminder of one of the ethics of a true chilli
lover: always tell your guests if a hot chilli is hiding in the food
you are serving!

Capsicum chinense

Madame Jeanette

SCOVILLE HEAT UNITS 100,000 – 350,000

SIZE
7 × 4 cm (2¾ × 1½ in.)

ORIGIN
Suriname

GROW
A flourishing grower in tropical climates, with an alternative red variety also available.

EAT
Make Madame Jeanette chutney with roasted tomatoes, peppers and shallots.

THE STORY GOES that Madame Jeanette was a famous Brazilian woman of certain repute, and there is certainly a seductive, curvaceous quality to the pods, accompanied by a sweet heat. Originally from the Republic of Suriname – the sovereign state on the north-eastern Atlantic coast of South America – the elongated Madame Jeanette (also known as Suriname Yellow) is a hot and fruity habanero-type chilli with subtle, sweet tropical notes of mango and pineapple. The heat affects the whole of the mouth, not just the back of the throat as with some chillies.

The pepper is prominent throughout Surinamese cuisine, with all its multicultural influences: East Indian, Javanese, Creole, Brazilian, Chinese, Dutch, Portuguese, Jewish and indigenous peoples. Madame Jeanette often spices up *pom*, the quintessential Surinamese dish made with chicken, lemon and grated *pomtajer* (arrowleaf elephant ear root – potatoes can be substituted). Hot Surinamese *sambal* – a rich chilli paste used as a condiment – can be made with Madame Jeanette (though adjuma peppers are also used).

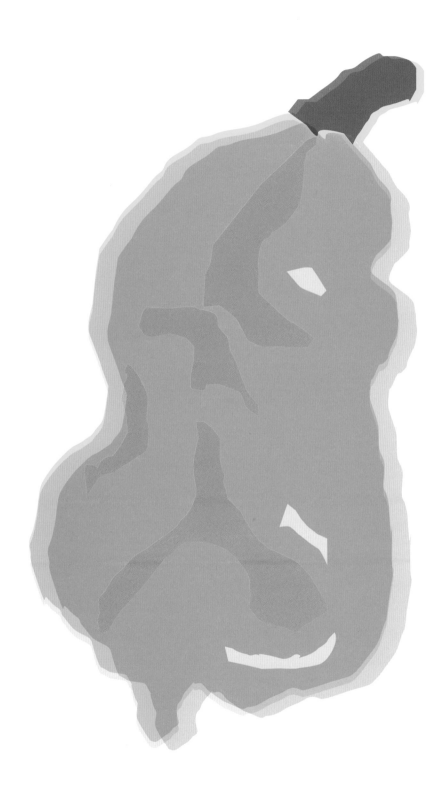

Capsicum chinense

Orange Habanero

SCOVILLE HEAT UNITS 100,000 – 350,000

SIZE
6 × 2.5 cm (2½ × 1 in.)

ORIGIN
Mexico and Belize

GROW
Now a much more commonly grown and loved chilli pepper, producing a shrubby bush up to 70 cm (28 in.) in circumference. Grow in a sunny spot and encourage more growth by picking the fruits just as they ripen.

EAT
Make orange habanero chutney. Master the art of the orange habanero salsa. Pickle in vinegar. Add to soups and stews.

RED AND GREEN habaneros are common sights, but the orange variety – grown in Mexico, Belize, Costa Rica and the USA – is the Rolls-Royce of the fleet. As with its relatives such as the Bahamian Goat (see pages 178–79) and Scotch Bonnet (see pages 190–91), the thin-skinned fruit is campanulate – lantern- or bell-shaped – with a pointed apex. The pods start out dark green and mature into a shiny, waxy golden-orange. This is a strong choice for an avid chilli eater and grower, offering vibrant flavour, biting heat and plentiful pods. It is great for adding to stews and curries, jerk sauces and chutneys, and it marries well with tropical fruit, lime, avocado, tomato, fish and grilled meats.

Habaneros have a history: the eighteenth-century Dominican priest Francisco Ximénez said that a single pod would 'make a bull unable to eat'. The epithet *habanero* means 'from Havana' as the pepper was believed to originate in Cuba, although its actual native home was probably the Amazon region. Because habaneros were distributed widely by the Spanish, reaching as far as China, early taxonomists mistakenly called them 'Chinese peppers', hence the Latin name for the species as a whole, *Capsicum chinense*.

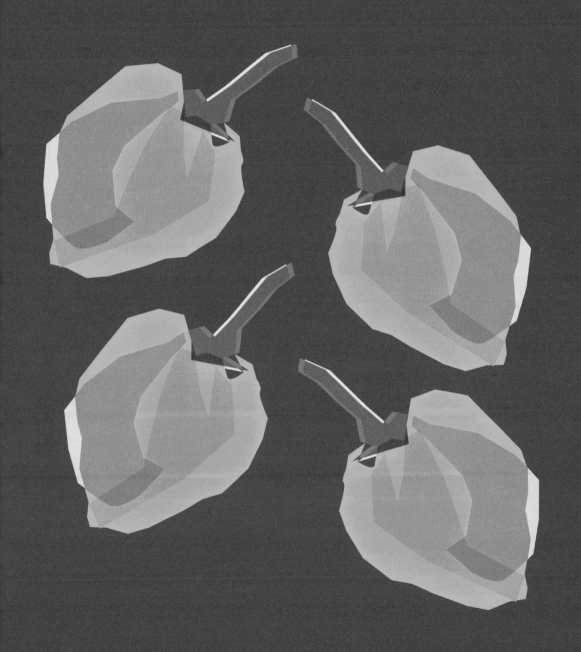

Scotch Bonnet

SCOVILLE HEAT UNITS 100,000 – 350,000

38
37
36
35
34
33
32
31
30
29
28
27
26
25
24
23
22
21
20
19
18
17
16
15
14
13
12
11
10
9
8
7
6
5
4
3
2
1
0

SIZE
4 × 3 cm (1½ × 1¼ in.)

ORIGIN
Caribbean

GROW
The plant grows to about
70 cm (28 in.) in a pot.

EAT
For a fish marinade, liquidize
Scotch Bonnet chillies with
garlic, oil, lime, fresh thyme
and parsley. Make Scotch
Bonnet chilli jelly or jam:
try pairing with either mint
or pineapple. Finesse your
Jamaican jerk sauce. Pickle.

THE SCOTCH BONNET is a hot, sweat-inducing chilli with a good long burn on the back of the throat. It is named for its resemblance to the tam o' shanter – the distinctive traditional Scottish flat woollen hat named for the hero of Robert Burns's poem of the same name. The chilli pod's four globular ridges look like the hat's seams, with the peduncle or stem as the woollen pompom or toorie that decorates the crown of the tam o' shanter.

Also known as the Scotty Bon, bonney pepper, Caribbean Red, Jamaican Hot, Bahama Mama or Martinique pepper, the corrugated Scotch Bonnet originates from Jamaica where it is grown extensively. Ripening yellow, orange or red, its flavour is sweet, stout and fruity with hints of tomato, apple and cherry (it is often paired with tropical fruit in Caribbean cuisine). Variants include the Tobago Scotch Bonnet and the Scotch Bonnet Chocolate, which ripens to a deep reddish brown.

The Scotch Bonnet is an important chilli in Caribbean and especially Caymanian and Jamaican cooking. Jamaican jerk spice, made with Scotch Bonnet and allspice, is used as a rub for meats before grilling. Scotch Bonnets also bring their distinctive flavour to other classic Caribbean dishes such as rice and peas, the coconut stew *rondon*, beef patties, ceviches and *escovitch* – a spicy, vinegary sauce with sautéed vegetables typically served with fish. Jollof rice, a West African speciality, is often spiced with Scotch Bonnets. British-Ghanaian food writer and chef Zoe Adjonyoh does a zingingly refreshing Scotch Bonnet ice cream, a reminder that chillies work well in desserts.

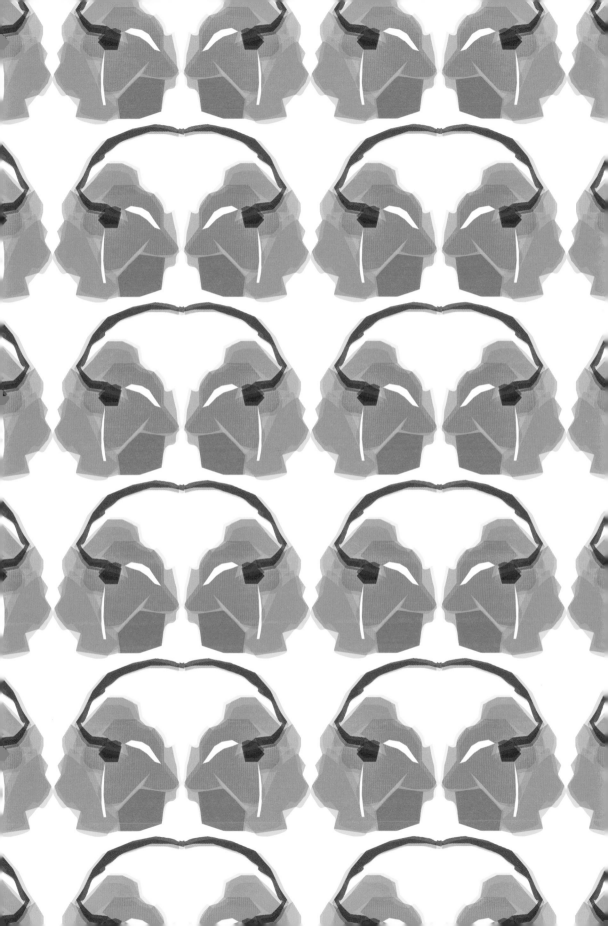

Hot Paper Lantern

SCOVILLE HEAT UNITS 150,000 – 350,000

SIZE
7 × 2 cm (2¾ × ¾ in.)

ORIGIN
South America

GROW
With heavier (and earlier) yields than other habaneros, the paper lantern grows upright well both in pots and in sheltered borders.

EAT
Light up any soup that calls for heat. Pair with carrots in a hot paper lantern sauce. Use dried in curries.

WITH ITS HOT and smoky, sweet and fruity flavour, these beautiful, ornamental pendent habanero pepper pods mature from lime green to vivid orange and bright red. The crispy, thin-walled, wrinkled pods are distinctive in shape – paper lantern, yes, but teardrop too – and the heat is ferocious for a beginner and satisfyingly challenging even for a chillihead (though without the overpowering habanero aftertaste). It means this is a great all-round habanero-type pepper for hotter sauces and fresh summer salsas with a kick.

Pink Tiger

SCOVILLE HEAT UNITS 400,000 – 500,000

SIZE
8 × 1.5 cm (3 × ½ in.)

ORIGIN
Italy

GROW
The plant grows strong, upwards of 80 cm (32 in.), with variegated leaves and a tendency to sprawl. Purple stems give way to great-looking, crinkled pods. Wear eye protection and gloves and work in a well-ventilated area when handling seeds or fruit.

EAT
Perfect for making an unusual homemade hot chilli sauce. Pair with tiger prawns, coriander and lime.

THE PINK TIGER is a hybrid of the bhut jolokia (also known as the ghost pepper; see pages 204–05) and the purple-chocolate-coloured Pimenta da Neyde (named after Neyde Hidalgo who discovered it in her garden in Brazil). It was developed in Italy in an attempt to make a purple bhut jolokia. That project did not succeed, but this blushing result is still very much worthy of attention.

The fruits turn from green to dark purple and ripen to peach or cream with purple and pink stripes or spots. (I presume the stripes give it its name.) There are many different colour and shape variations in the pods – a result of the hybrid being unstable – so if you grow this one, the appearance of the peppers that emerge will vary significantly depending on the amount of sun and the position of the plant. The heat of the pink tiger is high, but so too is its fruitiness, so this is an all-rounder: beautiful, hot and tasty.

Red Savina

SCOVILLE HEAT UNITS 350,000 – 577,000

SIZE
5 × 3.5 cm (2 × 1½ in.)

ORIGIN
California, USA

GROW
Harder to germinate,
though comparably easy for
a superhot, the beautiful
plants grow up to 1 m (3 ft)
tall with tubular bell-like
blossoms and sprawling
foliage. Wear eye protection
and gloves and work in a
well-ventilated area when
handling seeds or fruit.

EAT
Turn into a hot sauce.
Chop minuscule amounts
into avocado guacamole.
Add to a hot summer salsa
or jerk rub. Include in a
chocolate brownie recipe
for a pudding that packs
a punch.

THE RED SAVINA is the habanero-type pepper that until 2007
held the much-lauded title of world's hottest chilli pepper – as
stated by Guinness World Records at the time. It shows how
speedily superhot chillies have advanced in quite a short space
of time, given the now relative 'mildness' of its Scoville rating.
(Obviously this is still an extremely ferocious chilli pepper – take
care with it!) The Red Savina was eventually overtaken, first by the
bhut jolokia (see pages 204–05) and then by a succession of even
hotter superhots.

Selectively bred to be a larger, hotter habanero, with thicker
walls, the Red Savina was developed by Frank Garcia of GNS
Spices in Walnut, California. The story goes that after he had
finished ploughing a field of orange habaneros, one strange mutant
red pepper stood out; he pocketed it and eventually decided to
selectively breed its seeds.

The wrinkled pods of the Red Savina characteristically mature
to a shocking red. The heat is throbbingly intense and can cause
severe burning sensations; past the sting and the burn, a fruity,
smoky, apricot or even pineapple sweetness can be tasted.

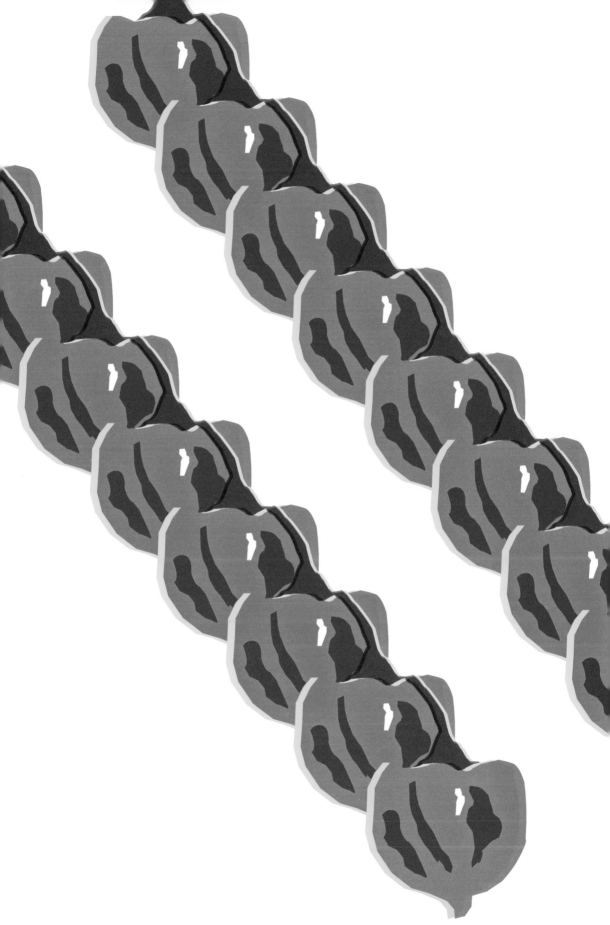

Capsicum chinense

Jay's Peach Ghost Scorpion

SCOVILLE HEAT UNITS 750,000 – 900,000

SIZE
10 × 2 cm (4 × ¾ in.)

ORIGIN
Pennsylvania, USA

GROW
Very productive plants, growing up to 1 m (3 ft) tall. Wear eye protection and gloves and work in a well-ventilated area when handling seeds or fruit.

EAT
Add sparingly – at most 1 chilli for 4–5 people – to curries and fruit chutneys. Or make a delicately blush-coloured but ferociously hot salad with peach, red onion and lime.

A CROSS BETWEEN the bhut jolokia (also known as the ghost pepper; see pages 204–05) and unusually light-coloured specimens of the Trinidad Scorpion, these plants produce elongated pendent pods that ripen from green to a striking pale peachy pink. The cross is new to the chilli world and has only recently been stabilized.

Officially called Jay's Peach Ghost Scorpion – the 'Jay' in the name is its developer, a farmer in eastern Pennsylvania – this extremely hot chilli grows into a wonderfully twisted, gnarly shape, often with spikes. Where most extremely hot chillies get darker the hotter they are, the opposite is the case with this one. Though extreme in heat, the flavour is floral (from the bhut jolokia) and slightly sweet (from the Trinidad Scorpion).

Warning – this chilli has an immediate and extremely hot and stinging burn on the inside of the mouth, at the tip and sides of the tongue.

Dorset Naga

SCOVILLE HEAT UNITS 900,000 – 1,221,000

49
48
47
46
45
44
43
42
41
40
39
38
37
36

SIZE
5 × 3 cm (2 × 1¼ in.)

35
34
33
32
31
30

ORIGIN
Bangladesh/Dorset, UK

29
28
27
26
25
24
23
22
21
20
19
18
17
16
15
14
13

GROW
Not one for the beginner
chilli grower, the Dorset
Naga grows best indoors.
It can become a large,
ungainly, prolific plant,
reaching 1.5 m (60 in.)
in height (it will be smaller
in pots). These plants are
late maturers and make good
autumn chillies, growing
well in colder climates like
the UK. Wear eye protection
and gloves and work in a
well-ventilated area when
handling seeds or fruit.

12
11
10
9
8

EAT
Good for chutneys, chilli
jams, sauces and curries –
but use only very sparingly.

7
6
5
4
3
2
1
0

ALTHOUGH THE DORSET NAGA is one of the hottest chillies in the world, it was bred in the south-west of England – not a region famed for its fiery cuisine. Internationally renowned chilli growers Joy and Michael Michaud, at the Sea Spring Seeds company on the Dorset coast, developed it from a Bangladeshi Naga Morich that they had purchased at a Bangladeshi shop in Bournemouth – so this chilli has more than one level of Dorset ancestry.

In 2006 the Dorset Naga was widely claimed to be the hottest chilli going – at the time of writing, the Carolina Reaper (see pages 210–11) is considered the hottest, though such records never last long in the chilli world. Its incredibly intense heat aside, the cone-shaped, wrinkled Dorset Naga offers a deep flavour, with a sweetness like a kick of orange or pineapple. The scent is fruity and strong, and the pods turn from an emerald green to lustrous red as they mature. The Dorset Naga is also prolific: the Michauds even nurtured a giant Dorset Naga plant (nicknamed 'Nigel') that produced 2,407 red pods in one picking! (And that did not even include the green ones.)

As with all superhots, wear gloves and eye protection when handling any part of the chilli – even a single seed can cause skin irritation – and be careful not to then touch your eyes.

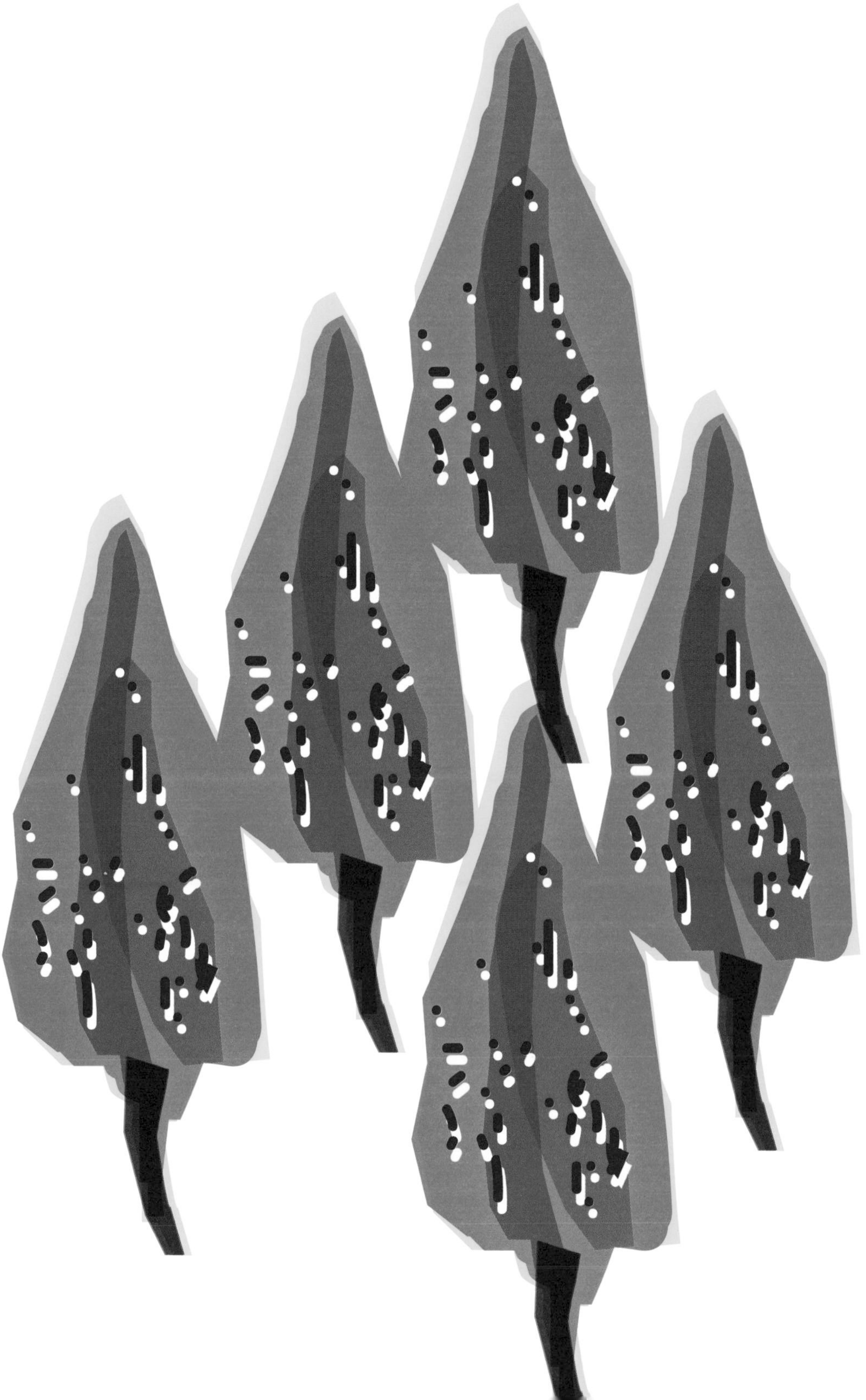

Naga Viper

SCOVILLE HEAT UNITS 1,000,000 – 1,382,118

SIZE
3 × 5 cm (1¼ × 2 in.)

ORIGIN
Cumbria, UK

GROW
It can take up to 100 days to grow a chilli-yielding plant from a seedling, and it is not yet clear whether this cultivar will be genetically stable enough for successful home growing. Wear eye protection and gloves and work in a well-ventilated area when handling seeds or fruit.

EAT
Add a tiny (tiny!) drop of Naga Viper chilli sauce to a tomato sauce or marinade.

THE PAINFULLY BEAUTIFUL Naga Viper was 'officially' the world's hottest chilli for a few months at the end of 2010, when it was tested by Warwick University – before being overtaken by the Carolina Reaper (see pages 210–11). A hybrid of three different chilli peppers – the bhut jolokia (see pages 204–05), the Naga Morich (see page 200) and the Trinidad Scorpion (see page 209) – it was created by British chilli farmer Gerald Fowler of the Chilli Pepper Company in Cark, Cumbria; he credits the county's famously wet weather for yielding such a scorching chilli, 270 times hotter than a jalapeño.

So blisteringly hot is this pepper – also known as The Terminator – that it is said to be able to peel paint and if you are attempting to try this one, be sure to have some dairy or bread on hand. Be aware, too, that the heat from this chilli will likely burn in the stomach long after eating, as its creator Fowler cautions: 'It numbs your tongue, then burns all the way down. It can last an hour, and you just don't want to talk to anyone or do anything. But it's a marvellous endorphin rush. It makes you feel great.' There is a growing trend for Naga Viper challenges in restaurants where the customer – who has most likely signed a legal waiver absolving the restaurant of responsibility – eats a Naga Viper sauce-covered speciality for 10 minutes, and refrains from drinking for a further 5-minute cooling-off period. Participants report burning throats, tearing eyes and heavy breathing.

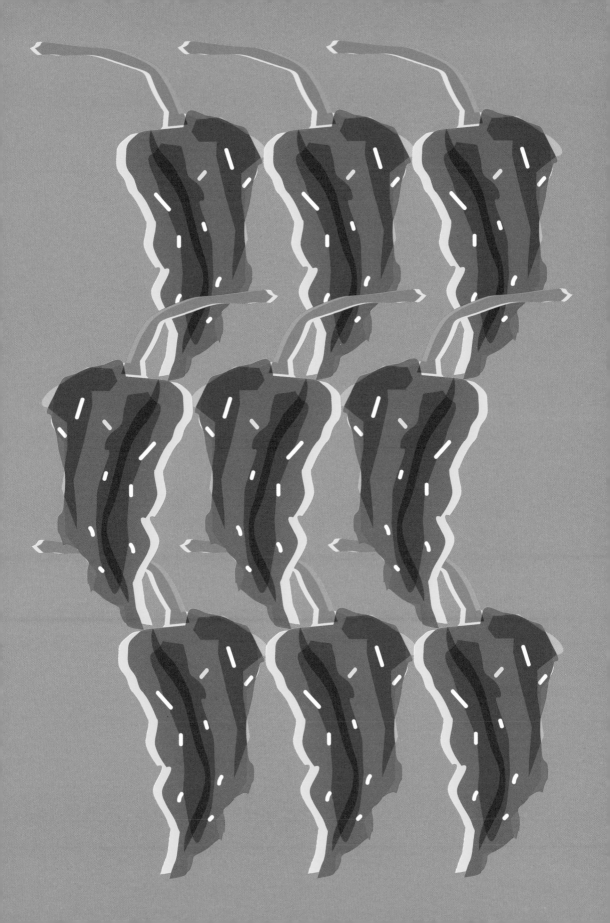

Bhut Jolokia

SCOVILLE HEAT UNITS 750,000 – 1.5 million

SIZE
3 × 9 cm (1¼ × 3½ in.)

ORIGIN
Assam, India

GROW
A trickier, more erratic chilli to grow, with a slow ripening time, requiring steady germination temperatures of 24–28°C (75–82°F). This is also a tall one, growing up to 1.2 m (4 ft), so staking is a must. Do not under- or overwater this fussy fireball. Wear eye protection and gloves and work in a well-ventilated area when handling seeds or fruit.

EAT
This one comes with a safety warning: use only a single chilli between 4–5 people in curries and sauces, pickles and chutneys.

ALSO KNOWN AS the ghost pepper, Naga Jolokia, Naga King Chilli or Red Naga, this thin-fleshed chilli (like its cousin, the Naga Morich, see page 200) is one of the world's hottest, with a persistent burn that can last hours after eating. The searing heat is matched with a fruitiness of flavour with hints of apricot or green apple. Bhut jolokia typically ripens from a lime green to a rich red (though some varieties are yellow, white, chocolate, purple or peach). The pepper has a distinctive wide shape and bulbous top with varyingly smooth and rough thin skin. DNA analysis has shown that this *Capsicum chinense* cultivar has some *Capsicum frutescens* in it, making it an interspecies chilli.

The chilli's history is as fierce as its heat. Anthropologist J. H. Hutton reported in the 1920s that the wives of 'head-taking' Naga warriors in Assam used the locally named bhut jolokia chillies to preserve their husbands' grisly war trophies. The Indian government has experimented with using bhut jolokia extract in non-lethal hand grenades and pepper sprays for riot control. In 2007, Guinness World Records certified that the bhut jolokia was the world's hottest chilli pepper; it was subsequently overtaken by the Carolina Reaper (see pages 210–11).

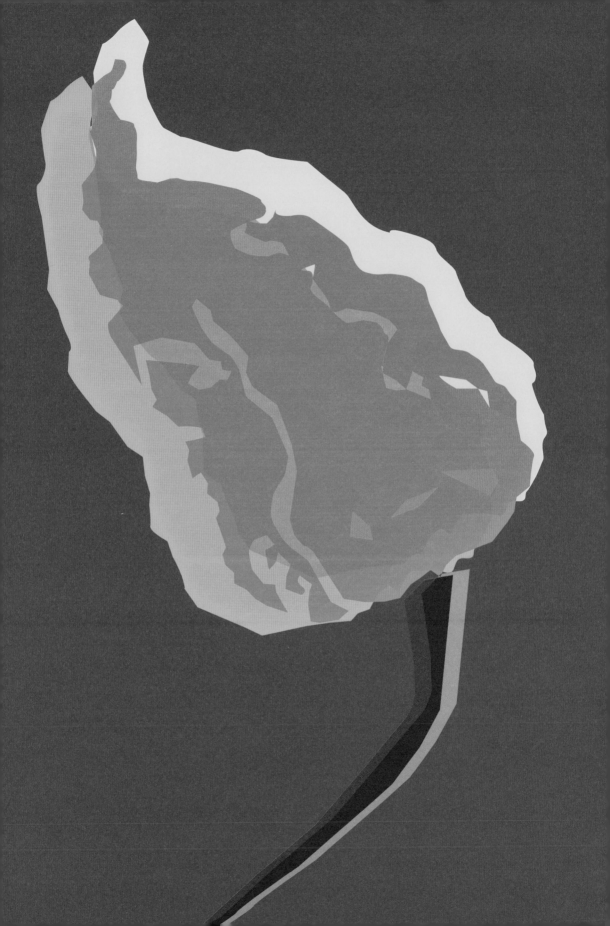

Chocolate 7-Pot

SCOVILLE HEAT UNITS 800,000 – 1.8 million

SIZE
6 × 4 cm (2½ × 1½ in.)

ORIGIN
Trinidad

GROW
Definitely one for the more
experienced chilli gardener
– especially given that
its seeds are difficult to
germinate and the plants
require a longer than usual
growing season. Wear eye
protection and gloves and
work in a well-ventilated
area when handling seeds
or fruit.

EAT
Only add a sliver if
incorporating this one into
soups or stews. Use a
few dried flakes to make
superhot brownies. If in
doubt, have a glass of
chocolate milk to hand
to counteract the heat!

ALLEGEDLY SO-CALLED because they are so hot that they
can flavour seven pots of stew, the little family of 7-Pot wonders
originates from Trinidad, where they have been a well-kept secret
until relatively recently. The 7-Pot (or 7-Pod) clan comes in all kinds
of shapes, colours and flavours: 7-Pot Orange, 7-Pot Burgundy,
7-Pot Yellow, even the Bubblegum 7-Pot and the Brain Strain 7-Pot.

The Chocolate 7-Pot, the hottest member of the clan, is a
thin-skinned dark brown pod with a pointed or inverted end and
rough, 'pimpled' skin. No genetic testing has been done on the
variety, which may in fact be the same as the similar-looking 7-Pot
Brown and Trinidad Douglah. They are difficult to grow and have
an extreme heat, but a beautiful and unusual skin colouring when
mature, and a sweet aroma when cut open.

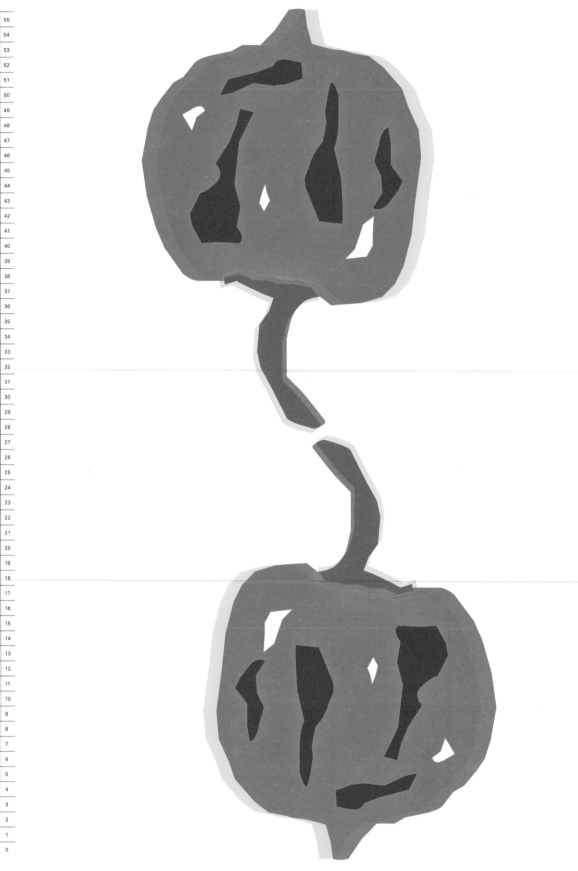

Trinidad Moruga Scorpion

SCOVILLE HEAT UNITS 1.2 – 2 million

SIZE
5 × 4 cm (2 × 1½ in.)

ORIGIN
Trinidad

GROW
Certainly not a novice chilli grower's starter plant. Extremely hard to start from seed, the Trinidad Moruga Scorpion requires patience while growing, taking up to 160 days to start producing pods. Wear eye protection and gloves and work in a well-ventilated area when handling seeds or fruit.

EAT
This is for expert chilli eaters only. For normal palettes, the Chile Pepper Institute's Paul Bosland says that 1–2 pods, used in tiny fragments, would be enough to flavour a week's worth of spicy meals for an entire household.

'WHEN IT COMES to bringing the heat, there's a new king of the hill.' So claimed the Chile Pepper Institute press release – based on a 'first-of-its-kind scientific study' by New Mexico State University in 2012. The study, which also involved the Trinidad Scorpion, the 7-Pot, the Chocolate 7-Pot (see pages 206–07) and the bhut jolokia (see pages 204–05), found that the Trinidad Moruga Scorpion exceeded two million SHUs (averaging at 1.2 million) – the first time the two million mark had been crossed. The study emphasized the difference between measuring a superhot chilli's average heat and its highest heat: chilli peppers of the same variety often vary in heat, even when grown in the same field or picked from the same plant.

Golf-ball-sized, with a long, stinging scorpion-like tail, the Trinidad Moruga Scorpion is named for the district on the island's south coast. It can be red or yellow (the latter cultivar was created by Trinidadian farmer Wahid Ogeer) and has thin, strangely pleated skin. Some experts, including Maricel E. Presilla, believe that it is essentially the same chilli as the Trinidad Scorpion, which DNA analysis has shown to be genetically indistinguishable (and both are open-pollinated landraces from the same area). Bearing a fruity, peachy, floral, herbal flavour under all that sweat-inducing heat, this is a mouth-igniting superhot whose excruciating burn continues to build long after swallowing – flushing faces and making eyes and noses water, judging from online videos of 'chilliheads' who have given it a go. For the warier curious, try a smidgen of the various commercially available Trinidad Moruga Scorpion hot sauces.

Capsicum chinense

Carolina Reaper

SCOVILLE HEAT UNITS   1,569,300 – 2.2 million

SIZE
7.5 × 7.5 cm (3 × 3 in.)

ORIGIN
South Carolina, USA

GROW
Start growing in an incubator, misting as it grows, and giving the plant as much sun and consistent heat as possible. Wear eye protection and gloves and work in a well-ventilated area when handling seeds or fruit.

EAT
If you dare, make hot jams, chilli powders, even Carolina Reaper vodka (be sure to follow handling instructions carefully). More than ever, take great care with this one and do not overestimate your tolerance for heat – this one really can slay you.

'EYES GLAZE. BROWS PERSPIRE. Arms flail.' So reads the description of this chilli on the PuckerButt Pepper Company website, developed by 'Founder, President, Mad-Scientist & Chef' Smokin' Ed Currie in the humid Deep South climate of South Carolina. Ten years in the making, the Carolina Reaper, which first appeared in 2011 under the strain number 'HP22B', was bred by crossing sweet habanero and Naga Viper (see pages 202–03) chillies. It was awarded the Guinness World Record for the hottest chilli in November 2013, defeating the Naga Viper.

If you manage to get through the heat – and that is a big *if* – it is described as having a sweet, fruity taste with a hint of cinnamon and even chocolate undertones. Indeed, Currie has now developed a darker, red-brown Chocolate Reaper (though it had not stabilized at time of print). Currie is also reportedly working on a strain called Pepper X, with an SHU value in excess of 3 million.

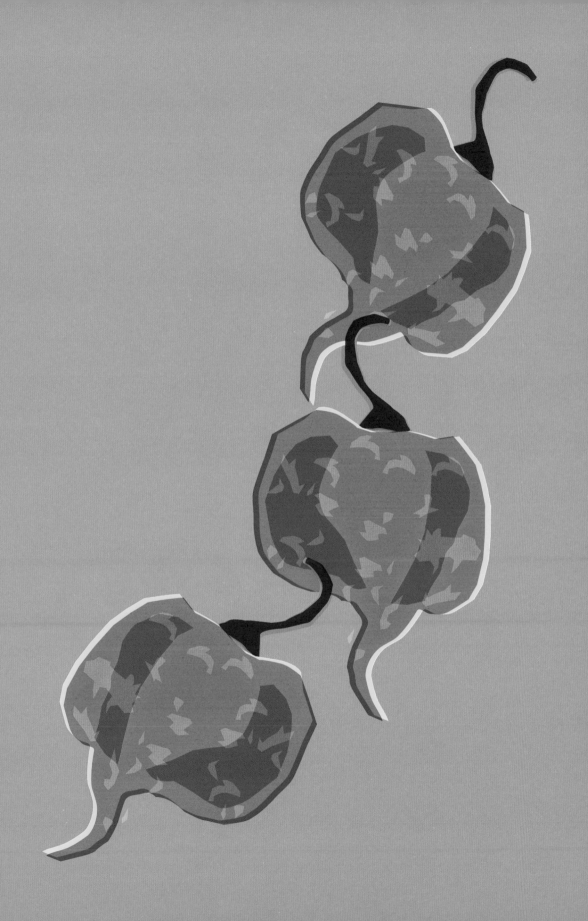

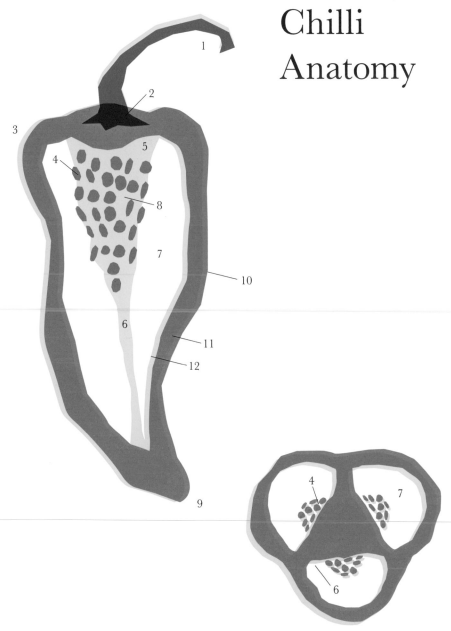

Chilli
Anatomy

Cross section of a capsicum fruit

1. Peduncle (stem)	5. Capsaicin glands	9. Apex
2. Calyx	6. Septa (partition)	10. Exocarp (skin)
3. Shoulder	7. Locule (lobe)	11. Mesocarp
4. Ovule (seed)	8. Placenta	12. Endocarp

Index of Alternative Common Names

Everyday Chillies

Growing chillies

Conditions needed	21°C (70°F) for seed germination
	Good level of all-round daylight
	Peat-free (non soil-based) seed compost

Good growing areas	Outdoors, greenhouse, conservatory, large window

Growing year	Early March	Plant seeds
	Mid March	Seedlings emerge
	End March	Pot small seedlings
	End April	Re-pot larger seedlings
	Mid May	Plant outside or in greenhouse
	Early June	First flowers appear
	Mid July	First fruits form (stake for support)
	End July	Pick first green chillies
	Mid August	Fruit turning red; keep picking
	Early September	Move outdoor plants indoors
	Early October	Keep plants sheltered
	Mid October	Bring inside; re-pot to overwinter

Chilli care checklist	Sun: good all-round light levels
	Warmth: at least 21°C (70°F) preferably 27–32°C (80–90°F)
	Fertilizer: high potash liquid chilli plant feed
	Water: do not waterlog, keep dry to yield hotter pods
	Humidity: moderate to high

Harvesting	Start as pods change from green to red, orange, purple...
	Pick off the chilli pod and stalk together
	Continue to harvest as the pods ripen
Easy, quicker growers	Apache F1, Hungarian Hot Wax, Jalapeño, Pimiento de Padrón, Prairie Fire, Serrano
Slower growers	Bhut Jolokia, Golden Cayenne, Hot Paper Lantern, Joe's Long Cayenne, Orange Habanero, Poblano
Ornamental growers	Hot Paper Lantern, Japanese Hot Claw, NuMex Twilight, Pot Black, Prairie Fire
Best for small spaces	Filius Blue, Lemon Drop, NuMex Twilight, Super Chile F1
Best for big bushy plants	African Bird's Eye, Brown Egg, Dorset Naga, Kpakpo Shito, Rocotillo, Peter Pepper
Best for indoor pots	Apache F1, Bhut Jolokia, Chiltepín, NuMex Twilight, Prik Kee Nu, Serrano
Best for cold climates	Bulgarian Carrot, Cyklon, Dorset Naga, Hinkelhatz, Ring of Fire

Chilli seed specialists

Sea Spring Seeds	www.seaspringseeds.co.uk
South Devon Chilli Farm	www.southdevonchillifarm.co.uk
Simpson's Seeds	www.simpsonsseeds.co.uk
Victoriana Nursery Gardens	www.victoriananursery.co.uk
The Chilli Pepper Company	www.chileseeds.co.uk
Baker Creek Heirloom Seeds	www.rareseeds.com
The Hippy Seed Company	www.thehippyseedcompany.com
Pepper Joe's	www.pepperjoe.com
Livingseeds	www.livingseeds.co.za
NMSU Chile Pepper Institute	https://chile.nmsu.edu

Using Chillies

Roast Place chilli on an open flame and allow skin to blacken (it will take about 3 minutes per side). Place in a plastic bag for 5 minutes to steam before peeling off skin. If using an oven, heat to 220°C (425°F), and place chilli on lightly oiled baking tray. Roast for 15–20 minutes.

Pickle Heat 250 ml water and 250 ml white wine/cider/rice wine vinegar to boiling with 25 g sugar. Cool slightly. Pour into warm sterilized jars (one method for sterilizing is to fill clean jars with boiling water and leave to sit for 30 minutes before emptying) stuffed with chopped chillies. Seal lids and store in a cool place for a month before eating; use for up to a year.

Sauce Blitz 10 large red chillies, 2 onions and 2 garlic cloves in a food processor. Heat in pan with a little oil. Add 2 tbsp sugar, 5 ripe tomatoes, 200 ml apple cider vinegar, 200 ml apple juice and a little salt. Liquidize before pouring into sterilized jars (see 'Pickle' note above for sterilizing tips and 'Chilli sauces' section for more inspiration).

Oil Prick dried chillies (never fresh – they will rot) and heat for 3–4 minutes in a pan of olive oil (add chilli flakes for extra measure). Decant into a sterilized bottle (see 'Pickle' note) and seal, storing for a few weeks before using.

Smoke In a lidded kettle barbecue, lay dried chillies on one end of rack, with hickory, pecan or mesquite wood chips at the other end, above hot coals (we are not cooking the chillies here, just smoking them). Cover with lid, allowing a small vent. Smoke for 4 hours and leave to cool. Freeze or store in sealed jars.

Freeze Freeze fresh pods from a bountiful chilli crop whole in plastic bags. Remove individual pods as needed and chop frozen – no need to thaw first.

Dry Longer, thinner cayenne-like varieties dry best. Leave on a tray in a sunny window, above a radiator, in an airing cupboard, or string up in a *ristra* and sun-dry outdoors in warmer climates. Alternatively, dry in an oven on low heat – 100°C (225°F) or lower – for a few hours, checking every so often.

Flake Put dry chillies in a food processor and pulse until they are roughly ground. If using a stored dried chilli, awaken its flavour by toasting on a skillet or in a medium oven for a few minutes.

Grind Grind dry chillies to powder in a spice mill or coffee grinder (see 'Flake' note about awakening flavour).

Chillies by flavour note

Citrus Ají Charapita, Chimayó, Chilhuacle Amarillo, Costeño (Amarillo), Datil, Fatalii, Lemon Drop, Pequin, Peruvian White Lightning, Petit Marseillais, Turtle Claw

Earthy Ancho, Chilaca, Chimayó, Guajillo, Ñora, NuMex Heritage 6-4

Floral Aci Sivri, Ají Amarillo, Jay's Peach Ghost Scorpion, Trinidad Moruga Scorpion

Fruity Ají Panca, Aleppo, Apricot Habanero, Bahamian Goat, Bhut Jolokia, Brown Egg, Bulgarian Carrot, Carolina Reaper, Cherry, Christmas Bell, Dorset Naga, Georgia Flame, Hungarian Hot Wax, Guajillo, Kashmiri Mirch, Madame Jeanette, Pepperoncini, Pink Tiger, Pulla, Rocotillo, Scotch Bonnet

Herbal Bell, Berbere Coffee Brown, Pimientos de Padrón, Trinidad Moruga Scorpion

Grassy Ají Charapita, Ají Panca, Chile de Árbol, Chiltepín, Costeño, Jalapeno, Pimientos de Padrón, Serrano

Nutty/Woody Cascabel, Chile de Árbol, Guajillo, Pequin

Smoky Ají Dulce, Berbere Coffee Brown, Biquenho, Brown Egg, Chile de Árbol, Chilhuacle Negro, Chipotle, Facing Heaven, Fresno, Hot Paper Lantern, Pequin, Poblano, Red Savina

Chillies for food

Salad Ají Amarillo, Ají Dulce, Apricot Habanero, Bahamian Goat, Bell, Christmas Bell, Costeño, Filius Blue, Hinkelhatz, Japanese Hot Claw, Manzano, Peruvian White Lightning

Salsa Georgia Flame, Paper Lantern, Pequin, Rocotillo, Sandia

Fish Ají Panca, Chilhuacle Amarillo, Chimayó, Datil, Fish Pepper, Lemon Drop, Prik Kee Noo

Meat Cascabel, Chimayó, Costeño, Pulla, Pusa Jwala

Stir-fries Cyklon, Facing Heaven, Goat Horn, Japones, Lemon Drop, Pot Black, Prairie Fire, Rooster Spur, Tabasco

Soups Malagueta, Mulato Isleño, Orange Habanero

Roasting Aci Sivri, Ají Amarillo, Anaheim, Cherry, Chilhuacle Amarillo, Manzano, Mulato Isleño, NuMex Heritage, Pulla

Frying Ají Amarillo, Bell, Cubanelle, Georgia Flame, Hungarian Hot Wax, Pimientos de Padrón

Smoking Guajillo, Jalapeño, Manzano, NuMex Primavera, Pasilla, Serrano

Paprika Cyklon, Georgia Flame, Ñora, Piment d'Espelette, Spaghetti

Chilli flakes Aleppo Pepper, Cascabel, Cheongyang Gochu, Chimayó, Dundicut, Guajillo, Japanese Hot Claw, Pequin, Peter Pepper, Ring of Fire, Sandia

Chilli powder Ancho, Berbere Coffee Brown, Japones, Kashmiri Mirch, NuMex Heritage 6-4, Pasilla, Pulla, Rooster Spur

Pickling Chiltepín, Fatalii, Goat Horn, Orange Habanero, Scotch Bonnet, Siling Labuyo, Tabasco

Stuffing Anaheim, Ancho, Apricot Habanero, Beaver Dam, Bell, Chilhuacle Amarillo, Cubanelle, Georgia Flame, Hungarian Hot Wax, Manzano, Petit Marseillais

Food for chillies

Fruit Apricot, Blood Orange, Blueberry, Grapefruit, Green Apple, Lemon, Lime, Mango, Orange, Passionfruit, Peach, Pear, Pineapple, Raspberry, Strawberry, Watermelon

Vegetables Aubergine (Eggplant), Avocado, Beetroot, Brussels Sprouts, Butternut Squash, Cabbage, Carrot, Fennel, Green Beans, Kale, Potato, Tomato

Larder Anise, Bacon, Bay, Cinnamon, Coconut Milk, Coriander (Cilantro), Egg, Ginger, Goat's Cheese, Mint, Pistachio, Rau Ram, Walnut

Chillies for chocolate

Ají Panca	Berry-like, good with acidic chocolate
Aleppo Pepper	Fresh and zesty, good with nutty chocolate
Ancho	Muted intensity, good with citrus chocolate
Berbere Coffee Brown	Fruity, smoky tang, good with milk chocolate
Cascabel	Coffee-like, good with roasted coffee chocolate
Chile de Árbol	Nutty, smoky, good with hot chocolate
Chipotle	Smoky flavour, good with dark chocolate
Guajillo	Peppery, good with all chocolate

Chillies for recipes

Aguachile	Serrano
Batair masala	Dundicut
Bigos	Cyklon
Birria	Cascabel
Causa rellena	Ají Amarillo
Calabacitas	NuMex Heritage 6-4
Chakhokhbili	Georgia Flame
Chicken basquaise	Piment D'Espelette
Chiles rellenos	Anaheim, Mulato Isleño
Chiles en nogada	Mulato Isleño
Chilli con carne	Ancho, Pasilla, Loco, Super Tramp
Escovitch	Scotch Bonnet

Jambalaya	Tabasco
Jollof rice	Scotch Bonnet
Minorcan clam chowder	Datil
Mole amarillo	Chilhuacle Amarillo, Costeño Amarillo
Mole costeño	Costeño Rojo, Guajillo
Mole de olla	Costeño Rojo
Mole negro/poblano	Ancho, Chilhuacle Negro, Chilhuacle Rojo, Guajillo Mulato Isleño, Pasilla
Muhammara	Aleppo Pepper
Pico de gallo	Fresno, Serrano
Pom	Madame Jeanette
Rogan josh	Kashmiri Mirch
Spaghetti alla puttanesca	Peppadew Piquanté
Torta ahogada	Chile de Árbol

Chilli sauces

Ají Traditionally mild, and recipes vary from region to region (it is made in Bolivia, Colombia and Peru), the sauce often contains tomatoes, coriander and onions as well as various ají peppers.

Biber salçası A rich red pepper paste used widely in Turkish cuisine, consisting of roasted peppers puréed and cooked with salt, lemon and oil.

Chimichurri With red and green versions, this Argentinian sauce is made of finely chopped parsley, minced garlic, red pepper flakes, oregano and white vinegar.

Chinese chilli oil Essential for Szechuan-style dishes, made with dried red chillies, mixed spices, ginger and toasted sesame seeds.

Gochujang A traditional Korean condiment used in soups, stews and bibimbap. Made in an earthenware pot that can be placed in a sunny place for fermentation, it includes barley malt powder, sweet rice flour, rice syrup, fermented soybean powder and chilli powder.

Harissa Hot and aromatic, spicy and fragrant, this hot red pepper condiment is widely used in North African and Middle Eastern cuisine. Additional ingredients can include fresh coriander, caraway seeds, smoked paprika, cumin and mint.

Jamaican Scotch Bonnet sauce A fruity, fiery sauce made with mango, mustard, brown sugar and white vinegar and used on summer barbecue marinades.

Louisiana hot sauce Hot and salty with a tang, usually made with cayenne or Tabasco peppers and vinegar. Perfect on seafood or in Cajun cooking.

Mazavaroo A Mauritian paste made with red chillies, garlic, ginger and fresh lemon.

Mole A general term for a variety of Central Mexican and Oaxacan sauces made from ground and roasted chillies, often incorporating sweet elements (such as dried fruits and chocolate), spices, tart elements (tomatillos or tomatoes) and thickeners (such as nuts, sesame seeds or cornmeal).

Nam phrik A key ingredient in Thai cuisine, nam phrik sauces are made with chillies, garlic, shallots, lime juice and fish sauce or shrimp paste.

Piri piri (or peri-peri) A flavourful African sauce made with bird's eye or malagueta chillies, garlic, paprika, olive oil and red wine vinegar or lemon juice.

Sambal A general term for a variety of chilli pastes and sauces made in Indonesia, Malaysia, Sri Lanka, Singapore and the former Dutch colony of Suriname. Most consist of crushed or ground chillies with additional flavourings such as shrimp paste, fish sauce, garlic, ginger, shallots, palm sugar, fruits, herbs and lime juice or vinegar.

Shito A Ghanaian hot black pepper sauce made with ginger, dried fish, prawns, tomatoes, garlic and chilli.

Sriracha A very hot sauce made from a paste of chilli peppers, vinegar, garlic, sugar and salt, named after the coastal city of Si Racha in eastern Thailand. Popularly used on pho and spring rolls.

Sweet Thai chilli sauce Called *nam chim kai* in Thailand, this is now an internationally popular syrupy sauce made with red chillies, rice wine vinegar, garlic and sugar or fruit juice (like apple).

Zhoug (or zhug) A hot and herbal spice paste made with coriander, cloves, parsley and green chilli and sometimes also caraway seed or cumin. Great with aubergine or eggs.

Select Bibliography

Anderson, Neil O., *Flower Breeding and Genetics: Issues, Challenges and Opportunities for the 21st Century* (Springer, 2006)

Andrews, Jean, *The Peppers Cookbook* (University of Texas Press, 2012)

—— *The Pepper Lady's Pocket Pepper Primer* (University of Texas Press, 1998)

Blythman, Joanna, *What to Eat: Food that's Good for your Health, Pocket and Plate* (Fourth Estate, 2013)

Davidson, Alan, *The Penguin Companion to Food* (Penguin, 2002)

DeWitt, Dave, and Paul W. Bosland, *The Complete Chili Pepper Book* (Timber Press, 2009)

—— *Peppers of the World: An Identification Guide* (Ten Speed Press, 1996)

DeWitt, Dave, *The Field Guide to Peppers* (Timber Press, 2016)

Floyd, David, *101 Chillies to Try Before You Die* (Cassell Illustrated, 2016)

Kennedy, Diana, *Oaxaca al Gusto: An Infinite Gastronomy* (University of Texas Press, 2010)

Kiple, Kenneth, *The Cambridge World History of Food: Volume 2* (Cambridge University Press, 2000)

Maguire, Kay, *RHS Red Hot Chilli Grower* (Mitchell Beazley, 2015)

McGee, Harold, *McGee on Food & Cooking* (Hodder & Stoughton, 2004)

Miers, Thomasina, *Chilli Notes* (Hodder & Stoughton, 2014)

Monaco, Enzo, *Peperoncino Amore Mio* (Rubbettino Editore, 2014)

Nickels, Jason, *Growing Chillies: A Guide to the Domestic Cultivation of Chilli Plants* (Jason Nickels, 2012)

Norman, Jill, *Herbs & Spices* (Dorling Kindersley, 2002)

Plunkett-Hogge, Kay, *Heat: Cooking with Chillies, the World's Favourite Spice* (Quercus Editions, 2016)

Presilla, Maricel E., *Peppers of the Americas* (Lorena Jones Books, 2017)

Weaver, William Woys, *Heirloom Vegetable Gardening: A Master Gardener's Guide to Planting, Seed Saving and Cultural History* (Henry Holt & Co, 1997)

Acknowledgments

The making of this book has been an exciting and sometimes alarming, but never lukewarm, experience. There are many people to thank for their contributions:

To the team at Thames & Hudson, for understanding our vision and helping to bring it to life with such care and attention: Lucas Dietrich, Avni Patel, Johanna Neurath, Rosie Keane, and extra special thanks to Flora Spiegel for her consistently generous guidance and attention to detail.

To Professore Massimo Biagi, inspirational chilli expert from Pisa, who sadly died before our book was published.

To Michael and Joy Michaud at Sea Spring Seeds on the Dorset coast, for giving us such a fascinating tour of their beautiful chilli farm and sharing their boundless chilli wisdom.

To Owen Taylor of the Philadelphia Seed Exchange and Truelove seeds for sharing some of his chilli stories from his inspiring work saving rare seeds.

To everyone in our studio, Here Design, for supporting us and helping bring this book to life, in particular Sakiko Kobayashi, Tom Key, Kara Johnson and Alex Merrett.

To Philip Cowell, special thanks for taking up the challenge (and the heat) of bringing order to the seething chaos of the world of chilli peppers.

Author Biography

Caz Hildebrand is a Creative Partner at Here Design, London, and the award-winning designer of best-selling cookbooks by Nigella Lawson, Yotam Ottolenghi and Sam and Sam Clark of Moro. She created *The Geometry of Pasta* (Thames & Hudson, 2010) with Bocca di Lupo chef Jacob Kenedy and is also the author and designer of *Herbarium* (Thames & Hudson, 2016) and *The Grammar of Spice* (Thames & Hudson, 2017).

A note of caution

We recommend that you always buy chilli plants, seeds or pods from a reputable supplier. Be aware that the heat of individual chillies of the same type can vary considerably, and some extremely hot chillies can resemble milder varieties. Never eat a whole chilli without tasting a small piece of it first. Chillies and their active ingredient capsaicin can irritate eyes, skin, genitals and mucus membranes and can cause breathing and digestive difficulties in some individuals if consumed at excessive levels. Use gloves to handle seeds of chillies over 30,000 SHUs, and do not then touch the face or eyes. Gloves, eye protection and adequate ventilation are always necessary when handling superhot chillies. The information provided in this book is not intended to be construed as or used as an alternative to medical advice. Speak to your doctor or another healthcare professional before taking herbal supplements or using chillies for medicinal purposes. The author and publisher cannot be held liable for any health issues that may result from the information presented in this publication.

An Anarchy of Chilies © 2018 Inkipit Ltd

Designed by Here Design

First published in the United States of America in 2018 by
Thames & Hudson Inc., 500 Fifth Avenue, New York, New York, 10110

www.thamesandhudsonusa.com

Library of Congress Control Number 2018932289

ISBN 978-0-500-02183-5

Printed and bound in China by C & C Offset Printing Co. Ltd